Crescent Color Guide to

PUPPIES

Crescent Color Guide to
PUPPIES

Angela Sayer

Crescent Books
New York

Copyright © The Hamlyn Publishing Group Limited MCMLXXXI

First English edition published by
Deans International Publishing
52-54 Southwark Street, London SE1 1UA
A division of The Hamlyn Publishing Group Limited
London · New York · Sydney · Toronto

ISBN 0-517-34183-2

This edition is published by Crescent Books,
a division of Crown Publishers, Inc.
h g f e d c b

Printed in Italy

Photography by Angela Sayer
(Tony Stone Associates: front cover, back cover, endpapers, title spread, contents spread and pages 7, 10, 19, 23, 27, 31, 37, 47, 59, 65, 67, 74, 79)

Contents

What is a Puppy?

A puppy is a young dog from the time it is born to the age of about one year when it is considered to have become adult. The new-born puppy is totally dependent upon its mother – helpless, blind and virtually deaf. Its muscles are very weak, and at this stage it is motivated by a series of involuntary reflex impulses from its poorly developed nervous system. This tiny creature is, however, a learning machine, for in the first twelve weeks of life it will undergo enormous behaviourial changes which will prepare it for a life quite different from the safety and confinement of the nestbox and its mother's care and protection.

Although no two puppies develop at exactly the same rate, and there is a great deal of overlapping in the various phases of behaviour patterns, observations have shown that these patterns do follow a sequence of innately timed events.

The first, or *neonatal*, phase of the puppy's development lasts from the moment of birth until the eyes open, and during this period the little animal only suckles and sleeps. The bitch–puppy relationship is crucial, and a close bond is established at the moment of birth when the bitch's first action is to lick the puppy, stimulating its breathing, and then eat the afterbirth. This licking and eating behaviour is continued for the first few weeks of the puppy's life, as the bitch keeps her baby clean, stimulates it to urinate and defecate and then swallows all the wastes, keeping the nest spotlessly clean.

Sleep takes precedence during this phase and a new-born pup may doze for more than ninety per cent of the day, waking only to be fed and cleaned. The little animal's movements at this time are governed by a series of reflexes, designed to keep it as close as possible to its mother for the warmth necessary for its survival for, at this stage, it cannot regulate its own body temperature. A good example of the automatic reflex actions of the very young puppy is the rooting reflex which happens when the bitch licks at the face of her straying youngster. This licking triggers off a contracting muscular action in the puppy's legs which causes it to crawl back to the safety of its dam's body. At this age the puppy moves by crawling with head

Right: Most of the small puppy's time is taken up in long periods of sleep.

Right: A young puppy is totally dependent upon its mother, and even after weaning, enjoys her companionship.

and body close to the ground, legs pushing in strong scrabbling movements at its sides. During the neonatal stage, puppies murmur and mew quite quietly, but by the ninth or tenth day of life more distinct protesting, and occasionally persistent, cries may be heard until the litter is about four weeks of age.

The puppy first opens its eyes at the onset of the second, or *transitional*, phase, generally between the tenth and sixteenth day of life. The eyes do not blink, focus or function properly at first, and the sight develops very slowly. Hearing is only weak at this stage too, and the rooting reflex starts to diminish. The immensely strong reflex sucking impulse, which causes the puppy to suck at virtually anything from the moment of birth, decreases noticeably at the end of this phase. The body and leg muscles strengthen and the puppy is able to move backwards as well as forwards, standing up sturdily on its legs.

At three weeks or so the puppy enters the third, or *socialization*, phase of its life. This is a very important period indeed, and lasts until the little dog is about ten weeks old. During this time it is weaned from its mother's milk and undergoes a great variety of learning processes. At the beginning of this stage, the puppy is at last able to control its own temperature and therefore needs less bodily contact with the bitch, and it also begins to show an interest in eating solid foods.

From three to four weeks of age, puppies sleep less and feed for longer periods. They also show the first signs of play behaviour. Life begins to take

Bernard at eight weeks is very responsive to the human voice and shows signs of being eager to please.

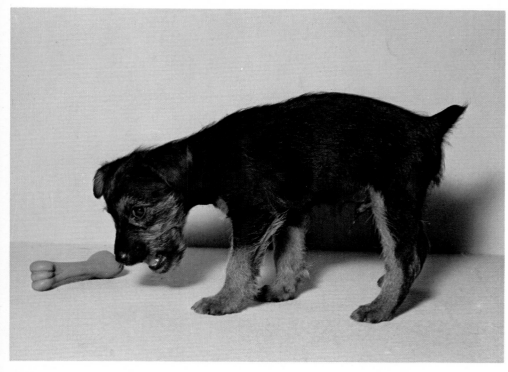

Once in his new home a puppy must be adequately compensated for the lack of playmates. *Charlie* enjoys rolling a huge, soft ball and chewing a specially hardened rubber bone.

on a more interesting pattern in which the puppies in the litter wake up, then try to leave their bed in order to urinate. They next want to feed and will react to and devour raw meat or food regurgitated by their mother, and will still suck strongly. After the bitch has cleaned and fed them, they will probably play for a while, taking time off occasionally to urinate or defecate. This pattern of behaviour should be carefully studied, for it is invaluable in the housetraining of the young puppy. The subtle cycle is quite constant – consisting of wake–urinate–feed–play–urinate/defecate– play–sleep. The puppy should be put on its tray, paper or earth as soon as it wakes, then again after it has been fed and has finished playing, whenever it pauses and looks pensive.

As the socialization phase progresses, the reflexes that the puppy relied upon in earlier days virtually disappear and its sleep periods reduce drastically. New abilities and reflexes are formed, conditioned by its immediate environment, and the little animal may begin to form strong attachments with humans or other animals. The puppy's brain continues its fast development rate and alpha rhythms, which show that the part of the brain concerned with vision has started to function, may be recorded. The puppy shows different types of brain activity between sleeping and waking. During this very important phase the puppy needs lots of human contact if it is to be easily trained at a later date. It is at this time that the little animal really begins to take full notice of its surroundings and its companions, plays properly and experiences various reactions and emotions, including fear.

A litter of puppies plays together quite happily during the socialization phase, but now and again a fight may break out between two or more of the siblings. This usually follows extra clumsiness or roughness by one of the puppies during play, and a short period of yapping, growling and sharp

This litter is almost three weeks old and the puppies are learning to relate to one another.

This small puppy is
looking a little
depressed at being
confronted by a
strong leather collar
and lead.

nibbling ensues. It is quite important that this is checked, however amusing
it might seem, for behaviour patterns tolerated at this age can easily become
patterns for life.

When scolded, the maturing puppy may pass a tiny amount of urine as
part of the submission reflex. If it feels excessively submissive, it will also
roll onto its back as well as urinating, but should not be punished for this
natural, inborn act of deference.

Although puppies are able to lap and eat from about the age of three
weeks, the bitch continues to feed her litter until it is six to eight weeks of
age, when weaning should be completed. This transition usually takes
place without any problems, the puppies being more than capable of eating
enough food for their needs. Once weaning is complete, puppies are ready
to go to their new homes. It is best to do this while the little animals are still
within the socialization period of development, for they are then fully
adaptable to change and particularly receptive to the formation of new and
close relationships with humans and other animals.

The fourth and final period in the development of the puppy is the
juvenile phase which lasts from the tenth week of its life until it is mature
enough to mate. By the end of this stage the puppy is considered to have
become a young adult dog.

Choosing the Right Puppy

The purchase of a new puppy needs serious thought and careful consideration. All puppies are appealing and difficult to resist, but you should never buy any animal on impulse. First you must decide whether you really do want a puppy, remembering that within one year it will have grown into a mature dog which should live for about another twelve or thirteen years. The dog must be housed, fed, vaccinated and cared for during that time, in sickness and in health, every day of every year, including during your holidays. Once you have taken on the responsibility of a puppy and accepted it into your home, the house will never again be quite as neat, clean and tidy, and your garden may suffer a little, too. On the credit side, a puppy gives you another dimension to your life, and for some lonely people a dog can be a worthwhile reason for living. A dog can be a nuisance, an added expense, a tie; it can also be a loyal companion and friend, a guard or, through the medium of the show world, a means of making many new friends and participating in a satisfying, enjoyable hobby.

Once you have decided to buy a puppy, and determined which breed or type will really suit you, be sure to obtain your pet directly from the place

Glowing with health, a Scottish Terrier puppy from the *Micanda* strain still has his ears folded down.

where it was born. You can find advertisements for all breeds in newspapers and dog journals, or you can write to breed-club secretaries for help with names and addresses of reputable breeders. The best pet shops often have lists of local breeders with puppies for sale and may be able to help you find, say, a cross-bred puppy or a Jack Russell Terrier. Your local veterinary surgeon might know of litters born locally if you just want an appealing pet but, if you want to show your puppy, go to the top breeders and be prepared to wait until the right puppy is available. You might be lucky enough to have the opportunity to give a good home to a puppy in need, one from a dog pound or rescue home, for example, but never ever buy one from a street market or from a puppy farm or dealer's kennels where litters from many sources are brought together for sale.

In Great Britain, Dog Breeders Associates and the National Dog Owners Association are two organizations which can help in finding the right puppy, while the governing body, the Kennel Club in London, and the American Kennel Club in the United States can also be of great assistance.

The sex of your proposed pet is an important decision that must be made, for making the right choice may have a bearing on your enjoyment of the animal as a pet in future years. Sometimes people decide that they want a puppy of one specific sex but, when they go to inspect their chosen litter, they find that all the puppies of that sex are the wrong colour. They may take one of the opposite sex, but perhaps regret their decision later on.

The male dog's outlook and attitude to life remains fairly constant once it has achieved full maturity, while that of the bitch may fluctuate with her hormonal cycles. She may be rather excitable or nervous when approaching her period of 'heat', and then have moods of depression when the season is over. Male dogs tend to be more outgoing and aware of life in general, while bitches often relate more to the family and the home. In the smaller breeds the differences between the sexes are less marked, while in the larger

Two puppies of similar size settle in well and may become devoted friends for life.

Young puppies, like this little Boston, benefit from exercise in the Spring sunshine.

A Lhasa Apso puppy is gentle, affection-ate and very intelligent.

One of the *Gable-down* Springer Spaniels, a cheeky and easily trained puppy, needing lots of exercise.

breeds the males are generally larger and more aggressive than their female counterparts.

Many people are put off the idea of keeping a bitch because they realize that she will regularly 'come into season', her period of oestrus, once she becomes adult at eight to twelve months of age. During her season, which lasts about twenty-one days, the bitch gives off a subtle odour which attracts male dogs in the neighbourhood, and she also has a discharge which may stain her bedding and the floor.

It is possible, however, to avoid this problem in the pet bitch by having her speyed. This veterinary operation is normally carried out after the animal's first normal season has passed, when she is one year old and has achieved full adulthood. Speying involves ovario-hysterectomy – the complete removal of the internal reproductive organs – after which the bitch needs a proper period of convalescence, followed by a normal life with a correct diet and amounts of exercise to avoid any chance of obesity.

Male dogs may be neutered by castration, but this is generally necessary only in extreme cases where a dog is quite uncontrollable or constantly roams the countryside looking for mates, thereby constituting a very real danger on the roads.

If you decide to buy two puppies, the question of their sex is even more important. Having a male and a female puppy together is fun, but you may not want to have your bitch speyed so that you may eventually breed a litter or two. You will then have great problems during her seasons, when you might have to board your male dog in kennels or have him castrated. Alternatively you may keep your male unneutered and spey your bitch. It is often said that bitches should always be allowed to have one litter but this is a fallacy, and many dogs live long and healthy lives without ever having pups. The best way to get good advice on neutering and breeding is to discuss matters with your veterinary surgeon.

Never buy a puppy as a Christmas present. The Christmas holiday period is generally a hectic one with lots of merrymaking, parties and visitors. A new puppy needs peace and quiet, and its digestion might be completely upset by having extra titbits of rich and quite unsuitable foods. It is also unwise to buy a puppy in the period leading up to your annual summer holidays; you will either have to take it along with you, giving rise to all sorts of problems with accommodation, feeding and exercise, or have to board the young animal at a formative and important stage in its life. It is far better to reserve a puppy and arrange to collect it after you arrive back home from your holidays.

Quite a lot of puppies are purchased by couples when the wife is expecting her first baby, and this usually proves to be a very good scheme. The wife is at home and can give a great deal of time to the puppy, starting its training and gaining its friendship, confidence and loyalty. The puppy will be almost trained by the time the human baby is born, and it will have settled into an adult pattern of life by the time the baby starts to toddle. A small puppy is not a suitable pet for a child aged between one and three years. It may make unhygienic patches on the floor where the child spends much of its play time, and the child will almost certainly play too roughly with the surprisingly frail little animal. A child of nursery-school age makes an ideal companion for a puppy; it can rest during the quiet of the day and enjoy a good romp in the late afternoon. It is obviously important to choose a puppy of a suitable breed as a companion for a child. Large breeds can be unintentionally clumsy and very small breeds can prove to be too delicate and prone to injury.

Most dog books discuss breeds by grouping them into categories as suggested by the various governing bodies associated with dogs. The Kennel Club which covers Britain has six groups: hounds, gundogs, terriers, utility breeds, working breeds and toys. The American Kennel Club has a slightly different grouping system with sporting dogs, hounds, working dogs, terriers, toys and non-sporting dogs. However, when choosing the right puppy, it is probably better to group the breeds by approximate size, for it is size, temperament and character that matter most in making the right selection. The large breeds are very impressive, but these puppies are often bought for the wrong reasons and insufficient thought is given to their needs. You should only buy one if you have plenty of room and can afford to provide the correct diet and care. Most big dogs have kindly natures but

Stelanjo Romulus is a smooth-coated Griffon Bruxellois, known as a Brabancon.

Left: Crossbred puppies can be handsome and very intelligent.

Above: The West Highland White is inquisitive and active, a typical terrier.

need firm, kind handling from an early age if they are to grow into safe, steady and obedient adults.

Very small breeds are often bought on impulse and they, too, have their special needs. Such dogs are quite cheap to feed, although the purchase of a toy-sized puppy will cost as much as, or maybe even more than, one of a large breed. If you prefer to have more than one puppy, two tiny ones are easier to house, feed and train than two very large ones. Little dogs might be treated as playthings by very small children, so with a young family in the home perhaps a medium-sized breed would prove best. This size has much to recommend it as a pet. It is large enough to avoid being trodden on or abused in any way, while still being small and neat enough to ride in the car, fit comfortably into most homes and is reasonable to feed.

If you can find the right sort of puppy fairly near to your home, so much the better, for it will be easier for you to maintain contact with its breeder, as well as being much easier to collect and transport back to your home.

The right way to buy a puppy is to contact the breeder and find out if and when puppies will be born or become available. You may be lucky enough to have chosen a breeder with a litter due, and then you will be contacted by telephone when the puppies have been safely delivered, to let you know if there is a suitable one of the right sex and colour. Once the puppies are three to four weeks old you may be permitted to visit and inspect them, and you may then be able to reserve the puppy of your choice. At this age the puppies will still be underdeveloped, but they should look clean and tidy with no sign of any unpleasant smell. They should all have their eyes open and be well fed and contented. You will have to rely on the breeder for advice on picking the puppy best suited to your needs, but you should be allowed to handle those you prefer and check that their tails have been docked if this is a requirement of the breed, that the dewclaws, found on the inside of the leg above the foot, have been neatly removed if necessary, and that the navel has healed and shows no sign of a hernia. The claws should have been neatly trimmed and the baby teeth should look evenly white and be sharply pointed. There should not be any sign of little black grits in the coat denoting the presence of fleas, and the insides of the ears should be slightly moist, clean and healthy-looking. Check the eyes: they should be bright and clear with no sign of any discharge in the corners. The nose should be clean, cold and damp, and the tail end should also be clean with no staining to suggest the puppy has suffered from a bout of diarrhoea.

The puppy should be well covered with flesh, but not too fat, and, unless it has been fed in the preceding hour, it should not have any sign of a distended stomach. A pot-bellied puppy could have worms; if it does, as well as its swollen abdomen, it will look rather thin with its ribs showing through the skin.

One other point to check is that there are no pimples, scabs or other lesions anywhere on the little animal's stomach or the inside of its thighs. Such areas could indicate the presence of skin diseases which might prove difficult to cure. Puppies do occasionally scratch and bite each other during play, but these marks are of no importance. Once you are satisfied with the condition of your intended pet, you should make arrangements to call again to collect the puppy when it is weaned and ready for its new home.

The earliest age at which the puppy will be allowed to leave its breeder is from eight to ten weeks, but if you want to buy a show puppy the breeder might want to keep it for several weeks more. This enables the breeder to ensure that you will get the best possible puppy, and you will expect to pay a higher price for the extra work and for such a dog of top quality. A pet puppy is best taken to its new home at about nine weeks of age when it is still within its very formative socialization phase and will adapt most rapidly to its new family and environment.

You will receive a signed form showing the ancestry of a pedigree puppy, and you should also get a registration card and transfer form. These documents are very important, but the breeder may not have received them from the registering body by the time you collect your puppy, in which case they will have to be forwarded on to you. Make sure that you do get a diet sheet and a receipt for the purchase price, and ask for convenient times at which you may telephone for advice.

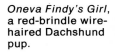

Oneva Findy's Girl, a red-brindle wire-haired Dachshund pup.

A trio of handsome Great Dane puppies from the *Nollybob* kennels.

SOME LARGE BREEDS

The tallest of all dog breeds is the IRISH WOLFHOUND, a gentle housedog but fierce when provoked. Although it is so large, the Wolfhound does not require any more exercise than a smaller dog, but does need unrestricted space in which to play during puppyhood. Intelligent and loyal, the Wolfhound is very good with children and its shaggy coat is quite easy to groom. A breed with similar lines and coat texture is the slightly lighter-framed DEERHOUND. This dog makes a devoted companion but needs lots of space and a good deal of exercise. The BORZOI is descended from the Wolfhounds of Russia. It is an aloof, tall and very graceful animal, and needs a considerable amount of exercise but, being a natural hunter, must be always kept under strict supervision. The beautiful long coat must be groomed daily to keep it looking at its best. The Borzoi needs careful training as a puppy and is not suitable as a child's pet.

Very tall and muscular but with a short smooth coat is the impressive GREAT DANE which makes an ideal family dog if you have sufficient space. Very easy to train and devoted to children and to other pets, the Dane needs surprisingly little exercise but regretfully has a short lifespan of only about ten years. The Dane is descended from the MASTIFF, an ancient breed used by the Romans in the arena and prized as a fighting and hunting dog as well as a guard. Today the Mastiff still guards well and becomes devoted to its owners. This breed is massively built and this can lead to problems with its joints; therefore a puppy must be quite sound at weaning and then reared and housed really well in order to prevent trouble occurring later.

The BULL MASTIFF resulted from initial crosses between the Mastiff and the Bulldog. It is important to pick one with the right temperament and to train it carefully if it is to be a family pet as well as a superb guard dog. Another dog of the Mastiff group is the ST BERNARD, a dog of very high intelligence which is easy to train, loyal and affectionate. Like the Great Dane this breed is not noted for its longevity, and it also does not need very much exercise. It has an interesting history, being famed for its rescue work in the Swiss Alps, finding and bringing stranded climbers to safety. The NEWFOUNDLAND is very similar to the St Bernard in build and is another traditional life-saving dog. Developed as a breed in the north-east of Canada, it has an inbred instinct to rescue anyone or anything from bodies of water. As a pet, the Newfoundland is very good with children and other animals. It needs daily grooming to keep the full coat in good condition, and plenty of regular exercise, preferably on hard ground.

The PYRENEAN MOUNTAIN DOG is another massive breed, dignified and rather aloof. It is a natural shepherd dog, developed in the Pyrenees on the Spanish/French border, but may make a suitable pet for those with enough space to house it properly. It is an excellent guard and does not tolerate strangers lightly although it gets on well with other family pets. An interesting product of the Newfoundland and the Pyrenean Mountain Dog is the handsome LEONBERGER, very rare outside Germany and bordering countries. An attractive light-coloured dog with dark points, the Leonberger was developed for pulling loads and guard work.

Far right: Old English Sheepdog puppies are very appealling, but grow into large, active dogs.

Elsa of Huntingrove, an Alsatian puppy at six weeks of age.

There are several other mountain dog breeds which have adapted to life as family pets. These include the ESTRELA MOUNTAIN DOG, which has existed for centuries in Portugal and is now becoming established as a show dog in other countries, and the BERNESE MOUNTAIN DOG from Switzerland. The Bernese is easily trained and loves everyone, including children and other pets, but it needs too much exercise to be suitable for life in towns. Like most of the other breeds of Swiss mountain dogs, the Bernese was used for draught work, herding and as a companion and guard.

Of all the large dogs originally used for herding, the most popular and well known is the GERMAN SHEPHERD DOG OR ALSATIAN. It is one of the most intelligent and courageous of all dogs and has been used in man's service for many years as police dog (sometimes trained to sniff out drugs), war dog (used by armies in warfare for many purposes, from carrying messages to detecting mines or injured people), as a guide for the blind, companion, guard and family pet. As a breed it is capable of arousing strong emotions and is generally either loved or greatly distrusted. The German Shepherd is easy to maintain in peak condition by correct feeding and adequate exercise, and responds so well to training that it makes an ideal subject for obedience work.

Belgium has produced four types of sheep-herding dogs with much the same build as their German counterpart. They are the GROENENDAEL, the MALINOIS, the TERVUEREN, and the rare LAEKENOIS, all named after villages in their native land. All are alike in needing plenty of open space and having excellent guarding potential, and are intelligent and robust and need little grooming. Differing very little in type, the four breeds are of distinct colours, the Groenendael being black, the Malinois dark fawn with a black overlay and muzzle, the Tervueren grey, fawn or red, also with a black overlay, and the Laekenois has a reddish-fawn rough coat, with a black muzzle and tail tip. The Belgian cattle-herding breed is called the BOUVIER DES FLANDRES, a large, impressive guard dog with a tousled and unkempt-looking coat. The Bouvier is not suited to city life as it needs quite a lot of exercise, but it does make a loyal and devoted one-man pet.

Best known of the French sheepdogs is the very heavily coated BRIARD. This is also an excellent guard dog and is happiest when it has plenty to do, such as working on a farm. Although the coat is so long, the Briard keeps itself remarkably clean and tidy and needs only a light daily brushing. Its British counterpart, however, does require extra work, needing a steel comb through its full coat. This is the OLD ENGLISH SHEEPDOG or BOBTAIL, one of the most reliable of breeds to have in a home with young children. The Bobtail needs plenty of room to exercise in the yard or garden, and is intelligent and easily trained as a puppy. The BEARDED COLLIE is also superb with children, being reliable and playful as well as readily trained. It is thought to have originated in Poland before being brought to Scotland, and does bear a slight resemblance to the Polish Sheepdog known as the OWCZAREK NIZINNY.

The ROUGH COLLIE makes an ideal family pet and is affectionate, loyal and easy to train. Despite its very full, long coat it is quite easy to groom and may even allow itself to be vacuum-cleaned. Although it loves children and is very obedient, the Rough Collie may be very wary of strangers. Of identical type and similar temperament, the SMOOTH COLLIE has a smooth, short coat which keeps soft and clean with very little grooming. It is much rarer than the Rough Collie which was popularized worldwide through the famous 'Lassie' films.

In Italy, the land of its origin, the MAREMMA SHEEPDOG has two names because two separate regions claim the breed as their own. This dog was not bred to work with sheep, but was developed as a strong and fearless guard to defend the flocks from the ravages of thieves, wolves and bears. Although the Maremma is strong, beautiful and intelligent, it can be difficult and headstrong during training. This dog needs a lot of exercise when young, but its virtually waterproof, white coat keeps remarkably clean with very little grooming.

From Hungary come three large and very unusual breeds. The first is a natural herding dog and an excellent guard, the intelligent HUNGARIAN KUVASZ. Its name is derived from the Turkish word meaning 'guardian of the peace', and it was prized as long ago as the fifteenth century for its

Right: *Sorrel*, a brown Dobermann Pinscher puppy, makes friends with *Alice*, a cream kitten.

Below: Dobermann puppies need firm, kind handling from an early age and make loving, loyal guards.

protective attitude, being used to guard Hungarian nobility against possible attack. Massively built and with an ivory or white coat of thick hair, the Kuvasz is slowly gaining in popularity outside its native land. Secondly, there is another white dog bred to guard flocks of sheep from raiders, but in the KOMONDOR the long coarse white coat naturally forms into thick tassel-like cords. This breed is very loyal and friendly to members of its owner's family but will rarely tolerate strangers. The coat is never brushed or combed and is very rarely washed because it takes a long time to dry. Komondor puppies are large and very active, thriving on lots of good food, exercise and methodical training sessions. The third Hungarian breed is a superb gundog and has a short, fine coat of a rich russet-gold. This is the HUNGARIAN VIZSLA, and its happy outward-going personality makes it an ideal family pet as well as a first-class worker in the field.

Known in the past as the 'grey ghost', the WEIMARANER is quite similar to the Hungarian Vizsla in conformation. It is an excellent gundog, once used for hunting big game, and has proved very successful in obedience work and as a police dog. The fine short coat needs little if any brushing, and is of an unusual silvery-grey colour. Like the Weimaraner, the DOBERMANN PINSCHER is a dog of German extraction and also makes an excellent police dog. Alert, intelligent and brave, it is one of the best guards in the world and will protect its home and family with its life if necessary. The short coat of the Dobermann needs very little grooming, but the breed needs plenty of exercise and careful, patient training in the early days.

Descended from German sheep- and cattle-herding dogs is the fearless GIANT SCHNAUZER, powerfully built, sinewy and almost square in outline. This breed is very easy to train, though rather slow to mature, and is excellent with children, being good-natured, protective and very wary and distrustful of strangers. Yet another German working dog of high intelligence and kind temperament is the sturdy ROTTWEILER which once pulled carts for butchers and cattle dealers and thus earned the name of 'butcher's dog'. A fine guard and good with small children, the Rottweiler has a short, easily maintained coat, and needs only moderate, regular exercise to keep fit. From southern Africa comes another dog willing to guard its family with its life. This is the light or red wheaten-coloured RHODESIAN RIDGEBACK, so called because of the strange distinctive ridge of hair that may be found along the forward end of its spine. This gives it the appearance of having its hackles permanently raised and is a breed characteristic which may be traced back to the animal's ancestors, the African Hottentot Hunting Dogs.

Three large British gundogs make up the Setter group, which derives its name from the traditional practice of training such animals to sit as soon as they had located game by scent and sight, when they became known as 'sitting' or 'setting' dogs. All the setters have elegant lines and long intelligent heads with very kind, gentle expressions. The IRISH SETTER is the finest boned of the three and is a rich chestnut in colour. Slightly heavier in build but of about the same height is the ENGLISH SETTER, generally white in colour with black, lemon, liver or tri-coloured markings flecked over the body and head. The GORDON SETTER from Scotland is a shiny black dog with striking chestnut markings. None of the setters are suitable as guard dogs, as they lack aggression and most of them are friendly to everyone they meet. They all need lots of regular exercise and careful grooming to keep the long silky feathering of their coat free from tangles.

As well as being an excellent gundog, the GOLDEN RETRIEVER must be recorded as the ideal large breed to be kept as a family pet. It has a delightful temperament and loves children. Its beautiful soft golden coat needs a little brushing each day, and the dog requires about an hour's steady exercise, as well as free playtimes in the garden if it is to keep fit and well. Very popular for work as guide-dogs for blind people, Golden Retrievers are very easy to train from an early age. The LABRADOR RETRIEVER is another ideal family dog as well as being a perfect gundog, originating in Newfoundland where it was used by fishermen to land their nets, swimming strongly and fearlessly through icy waters. This dog is generally black or yellow, but chocolate and other solid colours are sometimes seen. The FLAT-COATED RETRIEVER may be black or liver in colour. It is a gentle, hardy dog which retrieves quite naturally and is very easy to train for working or as a fine housedog.

Below: Irish Setter puppies at six weeks of age are quite irresistible.

Left: The English Setter pup is easy to train and is gentle but energetic.

Overleaf: Choosing a puppy can be very difficult, especially when they look as identically lovable as this litter.

21

Right: This little crossbred retriever pup soon learns to use the garden for his toilet needs.

Young puppies need a lot of play periods in order to develop mentally as well as physically.

Rather rare but very attractive, the CURLY COATED RETRIEVER is unusual with its black or liver coat of tight curls. The breed is extremely easy to train and very obedient. It makes a better guard dog than most of the other retrieving breeds and works well in all kinds of weather. It is an excellent swimmer, just like the CHESAPEAKE BAY RETRIEVER, a dog developed in Maryland in the United States from puppies of British origin. Although it is very good with children, this dog can be headstrong and difficult to train in the early stages. It is, however, a first-class working dog and quite unique with its slightly webbed feet and unusual yellow eyes.

The LARGE MÜNSTERLÄNDER is a multi-purpose gundog from Germany and looks rather like a setter in build but with a spaniel's head. Its head is black and its body white with patches, flecks or ticks of colour. A breed that needs plenty of exercise, the Münsterländer also makes a charming and affectionate pet – loyal, trustworthy and responsive to training.

There is some controversy regarding the origins of the pointing group of gundogs which find game by scent and sight and then freeze into a typical 'pointing' position. The English POINTER is a handsome dog with good bones and a well-proportioned body, usually white with either black, lemon, liver or orange markings. It is very easy to train and makes a good pet but it does require a great deal of steady exercise. The GERMAN SHORT-HAIRED POINTER is very similar to the English variety, while the GERMAN WIRE-HAIRED POINTER is slightly more aggressive than its smooth-coated cousins and is covered with a thick short coat of wiry hair.

Only one of the terrier group counts as a large breed. This is the AIREDALE, King of the Terriers, a sturdy dog once used extensively in policing docks and railways and during wartime, carrying messages and locating wounded men. As a guard it is practically unsurpassed and is very good with children. The wiry coat needs daily grooming and it will have to be expertly hand-stripped for show purposes.

It is very rare to find one of the pack hounds settling down to life in a normal home. These dogs prefer to live in company with the rest of their pack and are unsuitable as pets. However, some of the hounds that hunt by sight have adapted over the years and, if carefully trained and treated with understanding, can make excellent companions.

The PHARAOH HOUND is one of the most ancient of all recorded dog breeds. It is an affectionate and unusual-looking hound, full of fun and needing a lot of exercise. It does not generally care much for strangers, so makes a fairly good guard. It loves children and is very easy to groom. The IBIZAN HOUND is similar in conformation to the Pharaoh Hound and is a good gundog having been developed as a hunting dog on the mainland of Spain after being discovered on the island of Ibiza. Highly sensitive to loud noises and easily hurt by unkind words, the Ibizan needs a quiet, loving and understanding home.

One of the rarest of the sight hounds is the SLOUGHI, a smooth-coated, intelligent and gentle dog, tall and elegant. It is a very good guard dog and easy to train as a family pet as long as it has adequate exercise. In conformation it is virtually identical to the SALUKI, the gazelle-hunting hound of the Arabian deserts which has now become a glamorous show-stopper. The Saluki is very reliable in the home and with children, but it does have very strong hunting instincts and will not always come back when called. Another desert variety bred for hunting gazelles as well as wolves and foxes is the larger and taller AFGHAN HOUND, a close relation of the Saluki. This is a very independent and rather aloof breed which requires firm, loving care and daily, thorough grooming. Loyal and affectionate towards its owners, it will tolerate children but must never be teased. The GREYHOUND is rarely thought of as a pet, being bred and trained for racing on the track. However, Greyhound puppies are very quick to learn and can make excellent family dogs. Loyal and affectionate, the Greyhound is inclined to chase after things, rather like the Saluki, and must be treated with love and care, and never teased.

Needing a great deal of exercise to keep fit and occupied is the majestic BLOODHOUND. It is a breed of great character and charm, an excellent guard dog and very good with children. The red, black-and-tan or liver-and-tan coat is easily kept in good condition by the daily use of a hound glove, and the Bloodhound needs only quiet firm instructions – it must never be shouted at. Once used by the police for tracking purposes, this is one breed that has readily adapted to life in the family home.

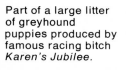

Part of a large litter of greyhound puppies produced by famous racing bitch *Karen's Jubilee.*

The ESKIMO DOG and the ALASKAN MALAMUTE are two working dogs of the Spitz group which have also become established as family pets. Both breeds have the typical upstanding coats and the curled-over tails of the group, and both make very good show dogs if properly trained as well as being fearless guards. Another Spitz is the ELKHOUND which needs plenty of careful training during puppyhood but then develops into a trustworthy and reliable guard, proving to be most reliable with small children. The CHOW CHOW is a remarkable breed, originating in China and reputed to be the original Lama's Mastiff. It is certainly one of the oldest of all the Spitz family and, with firm, strong handling, can make a good pet. Loyal only to its immediate family the Chow Chow makes a formidable guard. It needs about ten minutes' grooming each day and a wire brush helps to keep the thick coat in good condition. It has the distinction of being the only breed of dog to have a jet-black tongue.

The last trio of large dogs that we shall talk about in this book are old favourites. First, there is the STANDARD POODLE which really has everything a pet dog should have – brains, obedience, a good temperament and a great capacity for loving its immediate family and friends. The Poodle is very easy to train, but you must never make fun of it. The curly coat is groomed with a wire brush and may be clipped in the summer or for show purposes.

Next, there is the DALMATIAN, originally bred as a guard dog and expected to run between the wheels of a carriage. The Dalmatian will still guard well and still needs a considerable amount of exercise or it becomes bored and consequently rather mischievous. This breed is very loyal and good with children, but the spotted white coat needs daily grooming or may shed on the carpet.

Finally in our selection of large dogs we have the BOXER, a delightful animal that remains as full of fun as a puppy all its life, although it makes a superb guard and is very protective towards young children. Brave and easily trained, this dog was popular as a war dog and is sometimes used in police work and for guiding the blind.

Below: A charming Elkhound puppy, learning to 'sit and stay'.

Right: Dalmatian puppies need a lot of exercise and grow into large sturdy dogs, very reliable with children.

Right: *Adston Bourbon of Ockley*, an adult Puli with a typically corded coat, shares a joke with Puli pups *Ockley Sage* and *Ockley Mint*.

A sleepy, soulful Sussex Spaniel puppy, called *Quintic Seth*.

MEDIUM-SIZED BREEDS

The Spaniel family dates back to the fourteenth century when it was divided into two groups, Water and Land Spaniels. The neat little ENGLISH COCKER probably got its name from its skill in flushing out woodcock. An active dog that needs regular exercise, the Cocker Spaniel is affectionate and good with children as well as being an excellent gundog. The AMERICAN COCKER has a luxuriant coat and needs a lot of grooming. It is slightly smaller than the English variety and is adaptable and obedient. The WELSH SPRINGER, or 'starter' as it is known in Wales, is a tireless, lively dog, keen to hunt in water as well as on land. Puppies need careful training and discipline if they are to be family pets, and need a great deal of exercise. The ENGLISH SPRINGER is loyal, intelligent and loves children, making a good dual-purpose gundog and pet. The CLUMBER SPANIEL is the heaviest of the spaniel family and is attractive and brave, a slow, sure worker and a fine retriever. The FIELD SPANIEL is sensible and very affectionate, needing lots of exercise or work to keep it healthy. It has similar origins to the Cocker, and was not considered a separate breed until 1892. The SUSSEX SPANIEL tends to be a one-man dog. It was developed in southern England and was first shown in 1862. This glorious golden dog is now very rare which is sad, for it makes a wonderful companion and housepet.

Two small breeds of pack hounds fit into this medium-sized group of dogs, and both have adapted well to life as family pets. There is the BEAGLE, a merry affectionate little dog which makes a good all-round pet and a brave guard, and the heavier BASSET HOUND. Both breeds are inclined to have wanderlust, and the garden gate should always be tightly fastened. They are easy to groom and feed and get sufficient exercise by having the freedom of a medium-sized garden.

The BULL TERRIER is one of the most faithful of all dogs and very protective towards children. It is a hardy breed that needs plenty of exercise and firm handling when young. The STAFFORDSHIRE BULL TERRIER is also a first-class guard dog but needs careful training as it can be stubborn and loves to fight with other dogs. It adores the members of its own family and will never let an intruder into the house. The ancestor of both these Bull Terriers is the BULLDOG, an ancient breed once used in the sport of bull-baiting. This dog is courageous and intelligent, good natured and easy to groom, but it is not built for strenuous games or long walks and cannot stand extremes of climate. Two terriers of medium size are the SOFT-COATED WHEATEN and the KERRY BLUE. The former makes a gentle, well-behaved family dog which is defensive but not aggressive, and the latter is well suited to guard duties, and not averse to picking fights! It needs a lot of exercise and is excellent with children, and its coat needs daily brushing and regular trimming to keep it neat.

The medium-sized Spitz breeds fit comfortably into average homes. The SAMOYED is a beautiful white dog that originated as a sled dog in Siberia. Nevertheless it has adapted well to the fireside life and becomes devoted to its owner. The KEESHOND makes a good watchdog, having begun life as a barge dog. It usually has a very long lifespan and is a one-person dog that needs a lot of grooming. The NORWEGIAN BUHUND is another typical Spitz and, like the Keeshond, has its tail curled over its back. It was developed in Norway as a general purpose herding dog for cattle and sheep, but makes a good house pet. The FINNISH SPITZ, Finland's national dog, is home-living and sociable, and is generally reddish-brown in colour. The JAPANESE SPITZ is a natural herder, distrustful of strangers and tends to be a one-person dog. It has a profuse upstanding coat and the typical Spitz tail carriage.

Another dog with natural herding instincts is the HUNGARIAN PULI, an easily trained and highly intelligent dog with a remarkable corded coat. The Puli is very loyal, and makes an exceptional guard. The STANDARD SCHNAUZER from Germany is another good watchdog, being mistrustful of strangers. It loves games with children and is playful and affectionate.

For a medium-sized dog that combines the roles of affectionate pet and a useful performance in the show ring or on the track, there is nothing to beat the WHIPPET. Capable of speeds up to forty miles (64 km) per hour, it is a breed that needs lots of exercise and the correct diet. The short close coat is very easy to groom, but does not keep the dog very warm in inclement weather.

The BORDER COLLIE has become one of the most popular of all medium-sized dog breeds, as it is extremely intelligent and responds favourably to careful training. Perfect for obedience work, it is also good in the home, but needs lots of exercise and may become neurotic if bored.

Missie is a cute and affectionate Border Collie aged ten weeks.

SMALL DOGS

Most homes can find room for one of the small breeds of dog, and there is such an enormous variety of shapes, sizes, colours, types and personalities that there must surely be a small dog to suit everyone's taste. Little dogs must never be treated as animated toys, for most of them are just as intelligent as the larger breeds, and many of them are remarkably courageous for their size. While a tiny dog might cost as much as or even more than a large one, it proves far cheaper to keep and is much easier to house.

Perhaps the most popular of the Toys is the diminutive YORKSHIRE TERRIER, a game little dog with boundless energy. A good watchdog, its long coat needs careful grooming especially for show purposes. Another favourite 'tiny' is the CHIHUAHUA which comes in smooth and long-coated varieties. Both are fiercely protective, brave little dogs which hate the cold. They travel well and are very inexpensive to keep.

The smooth-coated Chihuahua makes an ideal pet for the town dweller.

Right: The Pekingese is another breed suitable for life in the city.

Similar in shape to the long-coated Chihuahua is the pretty little PAPILLON, a Toy Spaniel named after the French word meaning 'butterfly' because of the effect created by its large fringed ears. Long coated and white, with variously coloured markings, the Papillon's tail is carried over its back, just like that of the POMERANIAN, another happy and active little Toy breed.

Several of the Toys have very short noses, including the PUG, a gay little dog, affectionate, intelligent and good with children. It must not be allowed to get overweight, or overheated in warm weather, as it can have problems with its respiration. Also snub-nosed is the imperious PEKINGESE, once a royal dog of China. Although it gets along well with children, it is probably better suited to life with one doting adult, where it can be the centre of attention.

Both the LHASA APSO and the SHIH TZU are attractive long-coated Toys. Prize specimens of the former breed are reputed to have been given as gifts by the Dalai Lama of Tibet to visiting emperors and dignitaries, and in China were probably crossed with Pekingese, thus producing the Shih Tzu, sometimes called the Chrysanthemum Dog. From the same land came the TIBETAN SPANIEL, rather like a large Pekingese, and the TIBETAN TERRIER which resembles a small Old English Sheepdog.

A long-haired white Toy is the MALTESE TERRIER. Sensitive and sweet natured, it is extremely good with children but requires very careful daily grooming. The JAPANESE CHIN also loves children and probably shares a common ancestor with the Pekingese. It is, in fact, a tiny spaniel, black and white or red and white in colour, and is much tougher than it looks. Two other tiny spaniels are the KING CHARLES and the CAVALIER KING CHARLES. The former have short faces and are quite tiny, while the Cavaliers are a little larger and have longer noses. Both types love children and are very hardy; they make excellent house pets and love a daily romp.

There are two varieties of GRIFFON, the rough-coated Griffon Bruxellois and a smooth type called the Petit Brabançon. Both have amusing personalities to go with their appealing little faces. Always smooth haired is the neat MINIATURE PINSCHER, which may be black, blue or chocolate with clearly defined tan markings, and has a docked tail. Very similar in build is the ENGLISH TOY TERRIER, but this breed is always black-and-tan and is allowed to retain its natural tail. The ITALIAN GREYHOUND is an affectionate and obedient smooth-coated Toy dog. Very sensitive, it hates wind and rain and may need a protective coat in cold weather.

30

Right: An irresistible litter of apricot miniature poodles from the *Tiopepi* kennels.

Dachshunds make good family pets, affectionate, courageous and with a great sense of fun.

The incredible CHINESE CRESTED also needs protecting from the elements as it is an unusual, virtually hairless breed, very gentle with children. The very rare breeds always make good conversation openers, and one which never fails to attract attention is the AFFENPINSCHER with its unusual two-textured black coat and its monkey-like face. The LOWCHEN, too, causes great interest, as it is always clipped to look rather like a miniature lion. Careful clipping rounds the appearance of the BICHON FRISÉ which rather resembles a large powder puff, and the MINIATURE and TOY POODLES also need expert grooming and clipping to keep them looking as they should. Novice owners can have these specialist breeds regularly groomed and clipped by experts, or they may feel competent enough to learn the skilled techniques for themselves. It is important to understand the special needs of such breeds, however, before deciding to undertake owning one of them.

There are two WELSH CORGI breeds, the Pembroke with its docked tail and the Cardigan with its long tail. Both make devoted loyal pets and are fearless guards but need firm training when young. The DACHSHUND group has three coat types – long-haired, smooth-haired and wire-haired – and each type may be found in Standard or Miniature varieties. All dachshunds are brave, very affectionate and make good watchdogs, giving loud barks at the approach of strangers. Dachshunds need proper exercise, and they should be fed carefully or they may put on excess weight which gives rise to back troubles.

Lots of small terriers exist, and make lively pets. They need plenty of exercise and must never be expected to fit the role of lap dogs. The NORFOLK and NORWICH TERRIERS look very similar but the Norfolk has drop ears while the Norwich has pricked ones; both have short tails. The BORDER TERRIER is very active and sporty with drop ears and a long tail and the CAIRN is also very workmanlike and energetic, wiry and game for anything. The SCOTTISH TERRIER is black, wheaten or brindled and has a distinctive long, strong muzzle. This is a very brave little dog utterly loyal and a fine guard. Another terrier from Scotland is the popular WEST HIGHLAND WHITE which gets on well with other dogs and is particularly good with children. Its white coat must have regular grooming, however, and like the 'Scottie' it will need regular stripping. The SEALYHAM, which originated in Wales, is usually white, too, although other colours are allowed. This can prove to be an obstinate little dog but makes up for it by being very loving. Expert stripping is a must to prevent the coat becoming totally unmanageable. From the same country came the WELSH TERRIER, a true Celt in character and very like its larger cousins, the LAKELAND TERRIER and the IRISH TERRIER. All three are true terrier types and make lively sporty pets needing plenty of exercise and regular coat stripping.

The WIRE-HAIRED FOX TERRIER is another breed that needs hand-stripping two or three times a year, or more frequently if the dog is to be shown. It is a very smart intelligent terrier that loves to go hunting rabbits if the opportunity arises. The SMOOTH FOX TERRIER has similar conformation to that of the Wire-Haired, but is a separate breed that has been known for at least a hundred years. It makes an alert family pet with a smart appearance and its coat is very easy to groom and maintain.

Right: This almost adult Scottish Terrier brindle puppy is *Micanda Flash Harry*.

Below: The Miniature Schnauzer makes a good housepet and a fearless guard. This top-winning puppy is *Eastwight Sea Vision*.

Top: *Tango Jo of Ockley* is a small Boston Terrier puppy, intrigued with his new toy.

Above: Shetland Sheepdog puppies do very well if reared and raised in pairs, and play together tirelessly.

Immensely popular as a family pet and a working dog on smallholdings and farms is the cheeky JACK RUSSELL TERRIER, a very small dog with great bravery and a persistent nature, easy to train, feed and groom. Although not truly recognized, the breed was developed a century ago by a parson named Jack Russell, who bred the dogs to go to ground after foxes. Another dog used for finding foxes and badgers underground is the DANDIE DINMONT, an unusual-looking terrier with a large, impudent face, a long body and shortish legs. Its double-textured coat is kept tidy by normal brushing. The Isle of Skye in the Hebrides produced its own dog for hunting vermin. The SKYE TERRIER, when prepared for the show ring, looks far too glamorous to be a worker, but the little dog is hardy and tough and does not easily accept strangers in the home.

The MINIATURE SCHNAUZER is a very attractive breed. It makes a fearless guard, is intelligent and loves children. It enjoys romping in the garden but its coat must be kept tidy by regular hand-stripping. Needing very little grooming to keep its black coat gleaming is the SCHIPPERKE, originally a barge-dog. The name means 'little skipper' and the Schipperke is a Spitz breed with an inbred desire to guard its family and home. The BOSTON TERRIER is also easy to groom. It is a lively American breed which makes a wonderful pet and companion. The Boston is happiest when kept in the home and loves children, and the same applies to the SHETLAND SHEEPDOG, which looks like a miniature version of the Rough Collie. The 'Sheltie' is beautiful and intelligent and needs lots of regular grooming to keep its full coat immaculate.

Our final breed is the barkless BASENJI from Zaïre, well known for its gentle disposition and love of children. It is a very clean dog, often washing with its paw, just like a cat. This breed makes a wonderful and interesting pet but needs quite a lot of exercise to prevent it from putting on too much weight.

Caring for a Puppy

Before collecting your new puppy you should make a few adjustments to your home in order to make the little animal's transition period as painless as possible. Your garden or yard must be securely fenced and the gate latches checked. A 'Beware of the Dog' sign is also a good idea, even if the breed you have chosen is tiny and totally inoffensive. The sign will cause visitors to think twice before opening the gate, and they will be more inclined to shut it carefully behind them, preventing your puppy from getting loose and perhaps running into a busy road.

If possible, buy or construct a suitable playpen into which your pet can be placed when you need to confine it for any reason. The pen should be small enough to move around as you wish, but also large enough to contain the puppy's bed plus an adequate play area. By having its bed inside the pen, the puppy will soon come to regard the enclosure as its own territory rather than as a prison, and will never resent being confined for reasonable periods of time. Make a special box bed for your new pet. A thick cardboard carton is fine and can be totally sealed to make a safe 'cave' with a round hole in one side, just large enough for the puppy to walk through. A thick newspaper pad covered with, say, an old sweater should be put inside and the puppy will really appreciate the security and cosy warmth of such a simple bed. As the box becomes chewed or soiled, it is easily replaced, and your pup can graduate to a smart wicker basket when it has passed the destructive chewing stage.

Dogs kept together as family pets are often easier to manage if they are of similar breeds, like the Miniature Pinscher and the Chihuahua shown here.

Longcoated breeds need regular grooming to prevent hairs on the furnishings.

Make sure that all electric wires and cables are safely out of the puppy's reach and that there are no small objects around that it can pick up, chew or swallow. Put all houseplants up on shelves, well out of reach, and move any valuable furniture or rugs from the rooms in which the puppy is to be allowed to play. Have a good supply of newspapers on hand for training purposes, some suitable food- and water-bowls and a supply of foodstuffs that have been recommended by the breeder. Purchase an inexpensive adjustable puppy harness of suitable size, plus a lead, and you are ready to collect your puppy.

Try to collect your puppy as early in the day as possible, so that it has plenty of time to settle down before its first night away from its litter-mates. Take along a supply of newspapers and kitchen paper and protect your car seats with some old towels, for small puppies are often car-sick on their first journey. If you have a long ride back home, it is wise to telephone ahead and ask the breeder not to give the puppy its breakfast. Waste no time in completing the formalities of purchase, before setting off for home. Take the little harness you have brought and fit it on the puppy as a safety precaution, should you need to leave the car for any reason; it will help you retain a hold on your new pet. If you are buying a very tiny puppy, you can of course use a special carrier made of wicker, fibre-glass, perspex or wire-mesh, and line this with a soft pad of papers.

Above: Poodle puppies have naturally thick, curled coats and are regularly clipped from an early age.

Left: Cocker Spaniel puppies from the *Bidston* kennel understand simple commands from four weeks of age.

With a simple puppy
clip, silver poodle
Tiopepi Jim Dandy
is kept immaculate
with a daily brushing.

When you arrive home, do not fuss with the puppy too much. Give it a
small feed and some kind words, then place it in the spot you have chosen for
housetraining sessions. Then put it in its bed inside the playpen to rest after
the journey. A stone hot-water bottle wrapped in a warm pad is comforting
and may help the puppy to relax.

The puppy will miss its brothers and sisters at first, and may whine and
yelp. Comfort it from time to time, but be very firm about regular mealtimes
and rest periods, interspersed with play, until a set routine is established.
Start as you mean to continue, and do not allow bad habits to form. It is
difficult to resist a crying puppy, especially during the first few nights, but
it is healthier for the puppy, and you, if it sleeps in its proper bed and not in
yours. If it is warm, comfortable and properly fed, the puppy will soon
learn the routines of both night and day.

Using the breeder's diet sheet, feed your puppy correctly with the right
food at the proper temperature. Always prepare each meal separately,
and feed it on spotlessly clean plates. Remove any leftovers and dispose of
them. Stale food, or food straight from the refrigerator can give diarrhoea.
Make sure that you also provide fresh drinking water every day in a non-
spill bowl, and have this available for your puppy at all times. Check that
the puppy is able to drink from this bowl without having to dip its nose right
into the water. If it chokes every time it tries to drink, it may well become
reluctant to do so, and could develop digestive problems.

To carry your puppy, lift it carefully, encompassing its fore and hind
limbs to prevent it struggling and jumping out of your arms. Never lift it
with a hand under the stomach, or by the scruff of the neck. It is quite a good
idea to lift the puppy daily onto a table or bench for grooming, as you will
have to place it on a table for the veterinary surgeon when examinations or
vaccinations are necessary.

Whatever breed of puppy you have, it should be accustomed to a daily
grooming session from a very early age so that it becomes an enjoyable part
of the day's routine, building a bond between you and your pet. You must
be careful to use the correct types of brushes and combs for your breed.
Good quality grooming equipment is quite expensive but is a good investment and lasts a long time. Poor quality steel combs and wire brushes can
break the hair and scratch the animal's skin, and so may prove to be a false
economy.

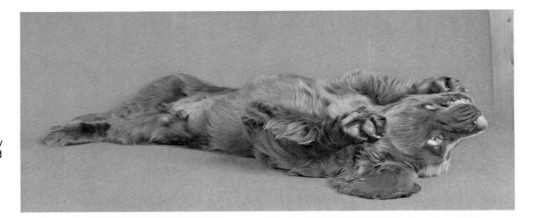

Right: Spaniel puppies are all very playful and respond to firm, gentle training with lots of praise for good behaviour.

Even as puppies, Pekingese are very well-behaved and dignified.

Brush your puppy all over, every day, paying special attention to the soft areas behind the ears, between the legs and under the belly. Smooth-coated breeds need a short-bristled brush, and are then rubbed all over with a soft pad of chamois leather, or with a special grooming mitten. Longer-coated breeds may have harsh, wiry coats or soft silky hair. The former benefit from the use of a steel comb, while the latter will probably need a wire brush or rake. In both cases it is advisable to work from the tail towards the head of the puppy, separating the hairs and teasing out any tangles. Such regular grooming keeps the coat in good condition and stimulates the circulation. It also enables you to notice immediately any attack by skin parasites such as fleas or lice, which can be instantly removed. Pest powders and sprays are not really suitable for use on young puppies as they can cause allergic reactions on the skin or gastric upsets if licked off the coat. Dry shampoo may be used to clean a dirty puppy. This is a powder sprinkled all over its body and massaged well into the coat. After a few minutes the powder absorbs all the dirt, dust and grease and is then thoroughly brushed out, leaving the puppy clean and fresh. Puppies should not be bathed unless really necessary, and only tepid water should be used to wash and rinse the little animal as quickly as possible before drying it carefully. Make sure that the brand of shampoo used is safe for small puppies.

During the grooming sessions, check your puppy's ears, eyes, teeth and nails and attend to them if necessary. Cotton buds may be used for cleaning dirty specks from inside the ear flaps and the corners of the eyes. Some puppies enjoy having their teeth cleaned but they should keep these immaculate themselves if fed correctly. Nails must be trimmed with clippers. Your veterinary surgeon is the best person to show you how to do this properly, and you must never try to use scissors which will merely splinter and break the nails. Always check your puppy's pads for soreness or thorns, and regularly check between its toes for scratches, embedded grit or small stones.

Your puppy may have started its vaccination programme before you have collected it. Puppies should be vaccinated against four fatal diseases: distemper or hardpad, canine viral hepatitis and two types of leptospirosis. One combined vaccine can protect against all these diseases and is generally given in two doses with a two-week interval between them. Your puppy must not be allowed to come into contact with other dogs until the vaccine has had time to work. Another disease, canine parvovirus, has caused deaths in puppies in recent years, and it might be wise to ask your veterinary surgeon's advice on vaccinations against this, too. You will receive official certificates of vaccination and should keep them safely on file along with your puppy's other papers. Most reputable boarding kennels require the production of a current certificate of vaccination before accepting dogs, and it is in your own interests to protect your pet against any unnecessary illness and the inevitable suffering and expense it brings. Vaccinations sometimes cause minor reactions in puppies, producing slight diarrhoea or sickness, general lassitude or drowsiness.

Good breeders always dose their puppies against roundworm infestation, but you should start a regular worming routine after consultation with your veterinary surgeon. Never give occasional doses of proprietary worming medicines or pills. Chances are that the dosage will be quite inadequate to clear worms, but sufficient to cause a severe gastric upset in your puppy's delicate stomach. Properly prescribed pills are necessary, the dosage calculated according to your puppy's weight. Correctly administered at intervals designed to slot into the roundworm's breeding cycle, these pills do their job efficiently and your puppy should show no ill effects.

You should accustom your pet to wearing a collar. Buy a soft, cheap collar at first, for the puppy will grow rapidly during the first few months in your care. Take it off every night and fit it again each morning. Make sure

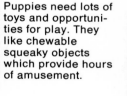

Puppies need lots of toys and opportunities for play. They like chewable squeaky objects which provide hours of amusement.

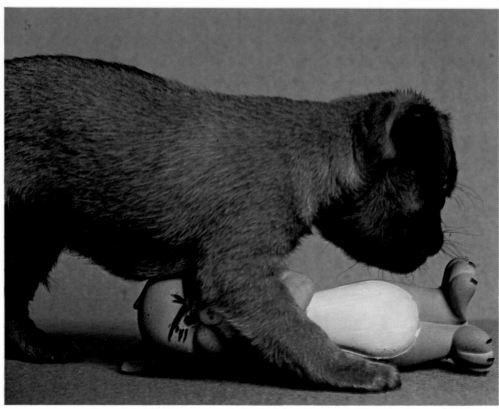

that it is never too tight or it may restrict breathing. Hard, unyielding leather collars or those allowed to get dirty quickly mark the puppy's neck, rubbing away the hair. You should attach a lead to the collar and let the puppy get used to dragging this around playfully as a prelude to lead training when, at first, the puppy will be allowed to walk where it wishes while you hold the lead. From time to time let it know that you have the end of it, then short walking lessons can commence. Ensure that the puppy accepts the discipline of the lead by ensuring that the lessons are fun and making a great fuss of the puppy every time it behaves well.

Try to avoid smacking your puppy; it is generally sufficient to use a stern but quiet voice to show your disapproval. Occasionally, a very large, strong or obstinate puppy might need punishing with more than the voice, and it is better to use a rolled newspaper to smack it. This will shock the puppy into obedience rather than hurting it. Most puppies really want to please at all times and respond quickly to the voice. Do not get into the habit of rewarding your puppy with chocolate drops or sweets or you will encourage the habit of begging for titbits which can be a nuisance.

At first your puppy will sleep quite a lot, and must have several small meals each day. You should spend time and care in housetraining the little animal, by observing its behavioural patterns and putting it outside or on its toilet area at the most obvious times. Make a great fuss of the puppy when it performs correctly, and make disapproving noises when it makes messes in the wrong place.

You should always address your pet by its name, which should be short and preferably of two syllables which helps the puppy to recognize it easily.

Play sessions are followed by periods of rest, during which the puppy should be left undisturbed.

Use simple words for training, always preceded by the animal's name to gain its attention. The first lesson is generally the 'sit' and, like all the preliminary teaching, should take place just before mealtimes, when the puppy is alert and waiting to see what you are going to do next. A stern 'no' is used for disapproval and a delighted 'good' – followed by its name – shows that you are pleased. You should teach the pup to 'come' during this stage and, after a few weeks, add 'stay', walking to 'heel' and perhaps 'go to your basket'. Never try to teach too much at a time and do not forget that you are dealing with a baby animal with limited learning ability, and one which tires quickly.

Play periods are very important in the development of a puppy's physical and mental powers, and should be encouraged but not allowed to go on until your pet is exhausted. Different breeds need differing amounts of exercise, so a little common sense is called for here. Children love to play with puppies, but the games must not be allowed to get out of hand. Puppies must never be pulled along on the end of a lead. They must not be woken up for a game, or allowed to become overheated and panting. They should not be carried around or placed on high places from which they might try to jump and be injured. Games should be designed to suit the type or breed of puppy that you have and should also be geared to the amount of exercise required. For example terriers and other strong, small breeds love to play tug-of-war games, while the gundogs soon learn to retrieve soft articles thrown for the purpose.

It is not advisable to allow your puppy to play unsupervised in your garden as it may find some of the plants to be quite irresistible. Puppies like

Play time again, this time having lots of fun with an old slipper.

Below: The Lhasa Apso needs quite a lot of exercise and must not be allowed to become bored, or it might get into mischief!

Left and below right: The Lhasa Apso and the Pekingese are two related breeds which have similar personalities and are well suited together as family pets.

to chew on all manner of new substances and some of the herbage can be dangerous. Daffodil, crocus and tulip bulbs are just the right size for carrying in a puppy's mouth, but if bitten and swallowed they prove quite poisonous, producing symptoms of excitability followed by severe gastric upset, collapse and coma. With bulbs about, it is best to move your puppy's playpen into the garden and put the little dog safely inside so that you are certain that it cannot get into any mischief. Some deadly common plants include buttercups, foxgloves, larkspur and peonies. Tomato and potato leaves are also toxic to puppies and some hedge clippings may make the little animal very sick if chewed. Indoor plants can be just as dangerous to your puppy, who might find the trailing stems of the philodendron too enticing to resist. Eating these and other related greenery could cause the mouth and throat to swell alarmingly, possibly causing asphyxia.

As your puppy grows past the baby stage, you can begin to train it properly. First of all, you must take time to learn something about the canine mind, and realize that it does not function in the same way as your own. Humans have the capability to analyse and collate complex thoughts and ideas, but dogs, with their vastly superior powers of sight, smell and hearing, are only equipped to learn and relate to simple ideas. The human, therefore, has to use his superior powers of reasoning to persuade the dog to behave and react in acceptable ways.

Even after centuries of domestication, today's dog retains many of the habits and behaviour patterns of its ancient wild ancestors. When it prepares to go to bed, for example, you may observe your dog turning round and round in a tight circle before finally curling up to sleep. A dog is a pack animal by nature and has therefore a psychological need to be part of a pack. The domesticated dog considers the human family as its pack and needs to be assured of its place in the hierarchy. A dog pack has a set pecking order from the leader down, and your dog will establish itself in its rightful niche from a very early age. By being, in your dog's eyes, the leader of its pack, you have a built-in advantage for being able to train the young animal. Most intelligent dogs really benefit from serious training sessions, which prevent them from becoming bored and mischievous.

By the time you and your puppy are ready for these sessions you will have established a happy relationship with one another. The puppy should trust you and be eating well-balanced meals at regular intervals. Apart from occasional minor transgressions, the young dog will be housetrained and clean, and it will have learned to differentiate between the pleased and angry tones of your voice. Even without really trying, you will have taught

your puppy quite a lot of basic training by this time. It will know its name and the command words that you have been using ever since you first brought the little animal home as a weanling pup. From two to five months of age, five-minute training sessions are sufficient to create a good working relationship between you and your puppy. In fact, they are more like play periods, and are designed not only to teach the basic words but to establish the animal's confidence in you.

At five months, the puppy may be fitted with a choke chain and a strong leather lead to be used during training. It should also have a correctly fitted collar of good quality leather to wear at other times and this should carry a disc or tag bearing its name plus your name, address and telephone number. This will help you to recover your dog in the unlikely event that it ever gets lost or strays from home. The choke chain must have fairly large, smooth links and should be of the correct length to fit snugly around your puppy's neck. Fine-linked chain must never be used as it is too harsh in action. To form a loop in the chain attach your lead to one ring and hold the lead end of the chain in your right hand. Take the ring at the other end of the chain in your left hand and let the chain links slide through this forming a loop. With the lead still in your right hand, open out the chain loop and slip it over the puppy's head. Correctly fitted in this way, the choke chain checks the puppy as and when you wish.

Overleaf:
Dachshunds seem
to do much better
when kept in pairs.
They are active,
lively and affection-
ate puppies.

45

For help and advice in training methods, it is a good idea to join a local dog-handling club. Here you will learn to train your pet in company and with expert guidance. Your puppy will already sit on command and will possibly retrieve small objects for you, so you must now concentrate on improving its 'heel' work. With the dog sitting on your left, the choke chain must be checked to ensure that it extends from your hand, over the puppy's neck and back underneath towards you, thus allowing the chain to go slack when no pressure is applied. The puppy soon learns that jerking forward or backwards on the chain causes it to pull tight. The lessons start when you walk forward slowly, saying 'heel' all the time, and jerking the chain every time your pet pulls too far forward or back. The chain only tightens when the puppy deviates from the action you desire, and causes the young dog to think hard about all its movements. Carry on for only a few minutes in the first daily lessons, and try to end each session when the pup has walked a few perfect paces.

When the heel work is going well, it can be interspersed with periods of halting to the 'sit' position, then going forward at 'heel' again. If the 'sit' is called for at random, the puppy will be alert and keenly waiting for the command, enjoying the challenge of being able to please you. Always give this lesson on the way to the park or area of your garden or yard where you allow the pup to run free and play as a reward for having behaved so well. During free play, your puppy will enjoy retrieving objects thrown for it, and you can incorporate lessons into the playtime, thus painlessly improving the retrieving technique.

Above: It is best to choose a puppy of a sensible, steady breed as a companion for an older dog. *Meme* the Jack Russell soon became very attached to Sussex Spaniel puppy *Quintic Seth*.

Left: The tricolour Cocker pup demonstrating complete obedience is *Inverneiti Gaiety Girl*.

Right: A Golden Retriever puppy is one of the easiest to train, being intelligent and always eager to please.

48

After your puppy has used up its abundant surplus energy in play, you should allow a short period, then introduce some 'sit and stay' lessons. It is best to have a helper to hold your pet's lead while you do the teaching. Put your hand under the puppy's neck and tell it to 'sit', then place your hand flat in front of its face and firmly tell it to 'stay'. Repeat the command several times while backing slowly away from your dog. If the puppy attempts to follow you, it must be firmly checked by your helper or, if you are working alone, you must take it back to the same spot and start again with 'sit'. After backing away for a few paces, bring your puppy to you by calling its name and the command 'come'. It is surprising how quickly puppies can learn this lesson, provided that you have lots of patience and keep very calm during the early stages. During this period of training, your puppy should start each session by practising what it already knows best. Any slipshod behaviour should be instantly corrected and the correction repeated until it is performed accurately and neatly once more. New lessons are introduced after some good behaviour has provoked a lot of praise, and sessions must never go on until you are tired and frustrated and your puppy is utterly bored.

Teaching the command 'down' is very valuable and follows on from the 'sit and stay'. When your puppy is in the 'sit' position, say 'down' very firmly and slide its front legs from under its body with your forearm. Do not allow your puppy to get up, but hold it in this position, repeating the command 'down' and, when it relaxes, give much praise. Many accidents have been avoided by the response of dogs to this command, and you should practise regularly until your puppy will go into the 'down' position at any time, even if it is in the middle of an exciting game and some distance away.

The basic training plans already outlined will suffice to turn your puppy into a well-behaved dog. Some breeds are always eager to please, while others might go through a rather headstrong stage as adolescents, trying you out with calculated acts of disobedience, just as a young wild dog would do. Dogs should never be beaten, for this rarely corrects bad behaviour and may produce nervous and neurotic dogs. Your puppy should be sufficiently chastised by a scolding voice, or a slap from a rolled-up newspaper.

When your dog is about one year old, you may want to teach it quite advanced movements, such as jumping obstacles and performing obedience tests. Who knows, with an intelligent pet and lots of patience you could end up with an Obedience Champion! Even if you do not aspire to such heights, a dog that is well behaved and responds to basic commands makes a much better pet than one which is too boisterous and uncontrollable.

Apart from normal training, you should teach your puppy a few manners. For example you should never allow it to jump up at any time. It might seem fun when the little dog is a few weeks old and is trying to get as near to your face as possible but, if this behaviour is not checked, it might not seem such fun when it is a fully grown dog with large, muddy paws, leaping up at you without warning. You should also teach your puppy to stay quietly on the floor of the car while it is in motion, and never let it ride along with its head out of the window as this can lead to serious trouble in the eyes and ears. Dogs have been known to get overexcited, too, jumping from moving cars to their deaths.

However much you love your puppy, you must be prepared to think of its well-being when you have to be away from home, on holiday perhaps or away on a business trip. You may be lucky enough to have friends or relations who will live in your home and care for your pet, but if not you must make arrangements for the young dog to go into kennel. Boarding

Holidays can create problems, but it may be possible to take your puppy with you, especially if you are camping.

Above: A pair of sweet and well-behaved golden Cocker Spaniels, *Bidston Barley Dancer* and *Sweet Candy of Bidston*.

Left: Miniature Schnauzers respond well to correct training. They have coats which need regular hand-stripping.

kennels are licensed by the local authority and must conform to certain standards as far as the provision of accommodation and hygiene is concerned, but even so, establishments vary a great deal in the service offered and the price you may have to pay. Try to find kennels recommended by friends who have received satisfactory care for their own dogs over a number of years, or your veterinary surgeon may be helpful in suggesting one. Having found a suitable establishment, telephone for an appointment to go and see the proprietor to discuss facilities and terms.

Kennels should be clean and spacious and there should be no strong doggy odours around. The proprietor should want to know quite a lot about your pet – its name, breed, age, sex and details of its vaccinations. You should also be asked about its favourite diet, special words of command that you use, fads and fancies, and if you want any special extras such as baths, extra grooming or the provision of extra heating. Good kennels will allow you to take along your dog's bed and toys and, if it is a long-haired breed, its own special grooming equipment. Make sure that the kennel does not accept unvaccinated dogs, and that your pet will have its own accommodation and not have to share with another dog. Make it clear that you would like a veterinary surgeon to attend your pet any time that it might seem necessary.

Never be persuaded to board your dog at a kennel just because it is the cheapest you can find. As with hotels, you generally get the accommodation and service that you pay for, and the cheapest kennel could prove to be false economy if you return to find a sick dog and a massive veterinary bill. When you have found a satisfactory kennel, make your booking early and make sure you build up your dog's health to peak condition before it is admitted. Go along on the arranged day, and be punctual for your appointment. Fill in your admission and diet forms, pay your bill and make your farewells as brief as possible. With luck your puppy's first period of boarding will be very short, hopefully only a long weekend; then, before it has a chance to get too depressed about being abandoned, you will return to collect your pet. Subsequent boarding periods may be longer, but your dog will always be confident that you will soon be coming back.

Most dogs board well and enjoy the routine of kennel life as well as the close proximity of other canines. It is essential that your dog's vaccinations are all up to date before it is boarded, and that it is not harbouring any parasites or incubating any disease. If you choose your kennel well, you will take in a happy healthy dog and when you return you will receive a fit and blooming one, freshly groomed and obviously great friends with the staff.

Sometimes puppies and young dogs misbehave in kennels, destroying their bedding and doing their best to escape. This generally happens the first time that they are confined, and is due to the fact that they do not understand that their incarceration is only temporary. If you are expecting to leave your young dog for a long stay in a kennel, try to arrange for a short preliminary board of two or three days prior to this, to give the animal confidence. Most kennel owners have the good of their canine guests at heart and will be only too pleased to help in such a conditioning programme.

Tiny breeds like the Chihuahua should be fed carefully to prevent overweight problems.

An A-Z of Puppy Health

A healthy puppy like this little 'Scottie' needs only mild antiseptic treatment for minor scratches.

ANAESTHETICS are used when surgery is needed for a puppy. Your veterinary surgeon will advise you of the necessity of withholding food prior to the administration of anaesthesia, and also on post-operative care.

ANAL GLANDS are a pair of blind sacs, each about the size of a small hazelnut, situated below and on either side of the puppy's anus. These glands secrete a paste-like substance with a strong and quite unpleasant smell, designed for use in territorial marking. The glands are rather inefficient at emptying themselves and sometimes become overfilled and distended, giving rise to pain and discomfort. This causes the affected animal to 'toboggan' across the floor in a sitting position. Other affected dogs lick incessantly at the area, or make sudden movements as though they have just been stung by insects. If your dog has regular problems with its anal glands, ask the veterinary surgeon to show you how to empty them yourself. Neglected and impacted glands are most painful and often lead to the formation of abscesses and a very sick, unhappy pet. The glands can be surgically removed if they present recurring problems, but preventive measures are really best. These consist of feeding your dog so that its motions are always well formed and passed daily, encouraging the regular milking-out of the anal glands in the natural way.

ANTIBIOTICS are drugs used in the treatment of secondary bacterial infections, not being effective against the primary virus. The veterinary surgeon prescribes the correct dose which must be given over a prescribed period of time, as it is the complete course of treatment which effects the cure. Never keep unused antibiotics in the medicine cupboard; they have

Below: A black Labrador enjoys his juicy fresh marrow bone.

Far right: Puppies with impacted anal glands may look dejected and pull their seats across the floor.

a limited lifespan, and out-of-date products may cause harm if given indiscriminately.

ANTISEPTICS should be selected and used with great care; some are very toxic, and others, for cleaning wounds, are destructive to cells and retard rather than aid healing. For first aid, cleanse wounds with well-diluted hydrogen peroxide, then rinse with salt water as a neutralizer.

ARTIFICIAL RESPIRATION may be given if your puppy has received some form of shock and appears to be dead. Lay the puppy on its side with its head lower than the rest of its body. Place one hand flat over the upper side of its abdomen and the other hand on the ribcage, then lean on your hands for a second or two before releasing the pressure. Repeat the movement rhythmically with a slight pause between each movement. Keep up the massage until professional help arrives, and remember that as long as you can detect a heartbeat there is hope of recovery.

ASPIRIN must never be given to your puppy as it is injurious to the mucous membrane of the stomach. Most human medicines are totally unsuitable for use in dogs, and your puppy should not be dosed with any substance without veterinary advice.

BITES from another dog can cause puncture wounds or tears. The area should be carefully cleaned and watched in case an infection introduced beneath the skin causes abscesses to form. Clip the hair away from the edges of such a wound and keep it open by daily bathing, so that it heals slowly from within.

BONES are not necessary for your puppy, although a beef marrow bone may be appreciated during teething. Poultry and chop bones splinter easily and can be fatal if swallowed, when the pieces may perforate the lining of the stomach.

CONJUNCTIVITIS is inflammation of the eye and may be caused by a number of factors, such as infection or a foreign body entering the eye. Bathing is necessary to clean away the discharges, followed by the application of an eye ointment, prescribed by the veterinary surgeon and squeezed along the inside of the lower lid.

CONSTIPATION is generally caused in the puppy by incorrect feeding and too little exercise. Check on the liquid content of the food and make sure that the puppy drinks enough fluids. Give extra warm milk and glucose and encourage more play periods. Liver has a laxative effect but you should not give too much. If there is no improvement, ask your veterinary surgeon for some laxative medicine.

COUGHS of the retching type sound as though the puppy has something caught in its throat. If there is no obstruction, then it could be kennel cough, an infectious bronchial virus which is dangerous in young puppies. Waste no time in seeking veterinary aid and, in the meantime, keep your puppy warm and quiet and allow it to lick a little honey from a teaspoon.

CUTS should be cleaned carefully, and pressure applied to such wounds to allow the blood to clot. Deep wounds might need professional suturing and such an operation needs to be carried out on the day of the accident. Prevent such accidents happening to your puppy by trying to foresee danger, and allowing it to play only in safe areas of the house and garden or yard where there are no obvious hazards.

DIARRHOEA is a condition in which liquid faeces are expelled at frequent intervals, sometimes accompanied by vomiting. The puppy may look generally unwell and should be kept extra warm. Withhold all food, giving only boiled water with a little added glucose and, if the condition persists for more than a few hours, get veterinary advice. Stress, over-excitement, an excess of milk or a change of diet can give a puppy loose motions, but

Right: Dogs with long ears must have them cleaned and inspected regularly to prevent infection.

Above: A little feral puppy like this has no protection from diseases such as distemper.

this condition, not to be confused with true diarrhoea, is easily put right by reversing the causative effect. By introducing peace and quiet or a bland diet, or by not giving any milk, the motions should quickly return to normal.

DISTEMPER is an infectious canine disease which can be prevented by vaccination. A puppy normally acquires this infection by breathing air contaminated by droplets sneezed or coughed out by another infected dog. The incubation period is thought to vary from five to twenty-eight days, but the infected puppy normally shows symptoms within ten days. The disease causes an initial rise in temperature, usually followed by discharges from the eyes and nose and accompanied by a cough. The puppy may also vomit and have diarrhoea. Within a short while, the little animal becomes thoroughly depressed and lethargic, and refuses to eat. The invading virus tends to attack the nervous system and causes fits and convulsions. Dedicated nursing, combined with constant, careful veterinary attention, are required if there is to be any hope of recovery.

EAR TROUBLES beset some puppies, especially those with long pendulous ears. The very structure of the dog's ears makes it vulnerable to invasion by parasites and, to prevent ear trouble developing, the weekly ear inspection is a vital part of canine care. Any rubbing or scratching of the ear should be investigated and treated without fail after a professional examination has been carried out. Neglected ear troubles can lead to infection of the middle ear and subsequent deafness, and may even cause loss of balance and co-ordination of the dog.

ECZEMA is a skin disease which may be caused by one of a number of factors including allergic reaction. Dogs sometimes develop dry skin conditions when fed a faulty diet. In any case, eczema should be seen by the veterinary surgeon to ascertain that the lesions are not fungal in origin.

ENTROPION is a condition in which the edge of the eyelid turns inwards and irritates the eye. It may be the result of disease in the puppy or may be caused by an inherited genetic factor. The condition may be cured by a surgical operation; if hereditary, the puppy should not be bred from.

FLEAS are parasites which live on dogs, biting through the skin to suck their blood. They can transmit several diseases and act as hosts to the tapeworm. The presence of fleas is indicated by tiny black grits, their excreta, found in the puppy's coat, particularly behind the ears and along the spine towards the tail, and also in the fine hair on the inside of the thighs. A suitable spray can be obtained from the veterinary surgeon, and the coat should be thoroughly combed daily with a fine-toothed steel comb made expressly for catching fleas.

FIRST-AID KIT for your puppy should include cotton wool and cotton buds; surgical spirit; Milk of Magnesia for stomach upsets; a bottle of veterinary-approved antiseptic lotion; professionally prescribed sedative tablets; worming tablets; pest powder; crêpe bandage; cotton bandages in two widths; lint or sterile dressing; roll of adhesive plaster or tape; blunt-ended tweezers; blunt-ended scissors (preferably with curved blades); and a pair of nail clippers. Keep these items in a safely situated cupboard or large tin box, and make sure that you and your family know exactly how to use them.

FITS, or convulsions, are sometimes experienced by puppies. They may be epileptic in origin and therefore hereditary, or they may be brought on by pain, a nervous upset or extreme fear. When having a fit, a puppy stops in its tracks and falls onto its side, tremors rack its body and it may pass urine and faeces. Keep it very quiet and, if possible, put a large dark box over the animal until the fit passes. Taking care not to get bitten, apply cold compresses to the animal's neck and head. Have the puppy thoroughly checked to make sure that the action of its heart is not impaired, and if the fits persist you must take veterinary advice regarding the puppy's future.

INJECTIONS are used to administer antibiotics and vaccines into the system of the puppy. Most injections are quite painless but, if you are upset by the sight and use of hypodermic needles, make sure that a nurse or assistant is available to handle your puppy when an injection is necessary, so that your distress is not transmitted to your pet.

LICE spend their life cycle on the dog. After laying their small white eggs, called nits, they firmly attach them to individual hairs. The adult insects are slow-moving and grey, slightly larger than a pin-head. Insecticidal shampoo will kill the adults, but an infected animal must be carefully and meticulously combed, too, to try and remove the eggs. It is normally necessary to give a series of shampoos to effectively cure a dog or puppy heavily infested with lice.

MANGE is caused by the presence of tiny mites. The *sarcoptic* mange mite burrows into the skin to lay its eggs and, in doing so, gives rise to areas of intense irritation. The sites chosen by this parasite include the ear flaps, hocks and upper limbs. The *demodectic* mange mite is microscopic and spends its life in the hair follicles and sebacous glands of the dog. Its presence is seen when scaly, discoloured patches devoid of hair appear in the dog's coat. Infection with mange is very debilitating, and the condition needs very careful and methodical treatment under veterinary supervision to clear the problem.

These semi-wild desert dogs show signs of mange around their heads.

MEDICINE is given to your puppy by pouring it slowly into the pouch formed when you pull out its cheek and lips, without opening its mouth. The little dog's head should be raised and it should swallow the liquid without too much fuss. You may find it easier to draw medicine into a disposable plastic syringe, the end of which can then be inserted between the puppy's teeth and the plunger gently depressed, expelling the liquid down its throat.

PAIN may be divided into three main types. *Internal pain* in the stomach, intestines or bowels causes the puppy to hunch its back and it will seem reluctant to move about very much. If you pick the little animal up, it might cry out, and you should take it to the veterinary surgeon for examination and possibly an X-ray to find the cause of the pain. Carry the puppy in your arms, or in a suitable container rather than letting it walk, in case there is some serious obstruction present. With *muscular and joint pain* the puppy refuses to walk and cries or yelps each time it moves. The puppy might also bite at certain areas of its body or legs as though it has an itch. Obtain professional advice as soon as possible and keep your pet quiet and warm. In *limb pain* the affected leg is held awkwardly or off the ground. If it hangs at an unnatural angle, it may be fractured, and needs expert attention without delay. If the puppy merely limps, the pain might be caused by a cut or strain, or there may be some foreign body, such as a stone or thorn, embedded in the pad or between the toes.

PILLS are given by placing them right at the back of the puppy's tongue. Open your pet's mouth with your hand over the muzzle, pressing the lips against its teeth. Pop in the pill and close the animal's mouth, keeping the chin raised and stroking the throat to induce swallowing. A titbit may be given as a reward for swallowing the pill; this is a good idea if you have to

Below: A puppy should be supervised in the garden and prevented from getting in contact with any poisonous substances like slug-bait.

Right: Always dry your puppy carefully after walks in wet weather to prevent the possibility of muscular or joint pain.

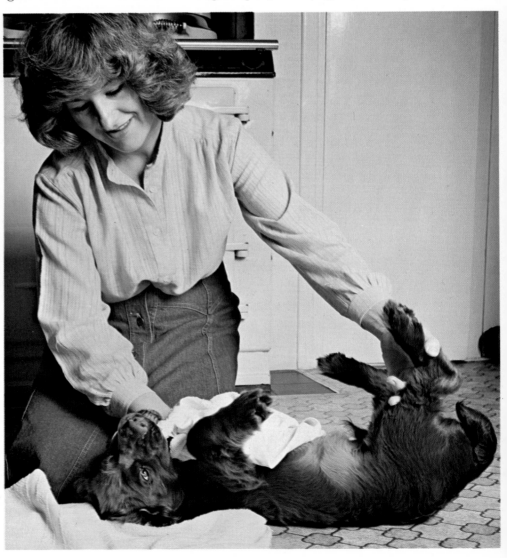

Ockley Sage, a Puli pup, shows what a healthy mouth should look like with no sign of pyorrhoea.

give a whole course of such treatment, when the routine can be turned into an enjoyable game for your puppy.

POISONING is quite common in puppies which will eat all manner of unsuitable things if allowed unsupervised play. They will readily eat slug bait and other pesticides if they find them in the garden. The former has no specific antidote to the metaldehyde it contains, and others may cause internal haemorrhages, so do not delay in seeking veterinary help. While waiting for aid, give the puppy a piece of washing soda about the size of a large pea; this will make it vomit and might bring up the poisonous substance.

POT BELLY in the puppy may be caused by malnutrition or a heavy burden of intestinal worms. Never buy a pot-bellied puppy but, if you decide to take on a waif in this condition, first ask your veterinary surgeon to determine the cause and treat it carefully, then feed the pup small, good-quality meals at short intervals until it develops muscle tone and a normal shape.

PYORRHOEA is an unpleasant condition of the mouth caused by an accumulation of tartar on the teeth which presses on the gums, causing inflammation and pain. The first signs of this condition include offensive breath and discoloration of the teeth. It is often caused by feeding soft food and may be prevented by giving your puppy hard biscuits and rawhide chews to gnaw on from an early age.

RINGWORM is a fungal disease and is very contagious to humans as well as to dogs. Patches form on the skin and are so irritating that the infected dog scratches constantly and loses condition through lack of sleep. The scratched lesions may weep and become infected. Specialist treatment is needed and careful nursing essential to prevent the spread of this unpleasant disease.

SHOCK must be treated with quiet care until veterinary help arrives. Dogs may suffer shock after any accidents involving internal and external bleeding, and sometimes after surgical operations. Never try to force brandy or any other liquid down the throat of an unconscious dog, and take care that you do not get bitten if the uncoordinated animal starts to come round.

SORE THROAT is indicated when the puppy continuously lifts its head high and appears to be looking at the ceiling. On examination the lining of the throat may look red and sore. Keep the puppy quiet and allow it to lick honey from a teaspoon to soothe the throat. Try to prevent it from barking, and watch out for any other symptoms which could herald the onset of a connected illness.

TEMPERATURE. The normal temperature of a puppy at rest is 101°F (38·6°C) and is taken by inserting a heavy-duty veterinary thermometer just inside its rectum. The easiest way to do this is to have someone hold the puppy, lying comfortably on its side on a table, and then insert the lubricated end of the thermometer into place, holding it there for two minutes, before reading off the scale.

TICKS may be picked up in the spring and autumn when the puppy plays among long grass in the countryside. These parasites are grey in colour and attach themselves by strong mouthparts to the animal's skin. Engorging themselves on blood, they grow rapidly, sometimes to the size and shape of a baked bean, when they may release their hold and drop off the animal. To remove a tick, it is extremely important to relax the creature's jaws and this may be done by swabbing around its mouthparts with surgical spirit. Once the tick relaxes its jaws, it may be lifted away with tweezers and destroyed.

WORMS can be controlled by regular dosings of the correct vermifuge, available from your veterinary surgeon. Dogs can suffer from various types of worms and a microscopic examination of an animal's faeces will determine the presence and species of the parasites. The roundworm commonly found in dogs is *Toxocara canis*. Its sticky eggs, passed by infected dogs, may be inadvertently ingested, with unpleasant results, by humans. It is important to wash your hands after handling your puppy, and to maintain sensible levels of hygiene in the home. Routine worming doses may be given to young puppies, and adult dogs may also be wormed at regular intervals each year.

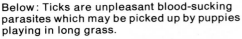

Below: Ticks are unpleasant blood-sucking parasites which may be picked up by puppies playing in long grass.

Below: This Elkhound is an example of a puppy in excellent health.

Right: *Adrian* loves his puppy but knows that he must always wash his hands after their play sessions.

An undernourished feral puppy suffering from a high temperature.

A listless puppy may be suffering from worms, and all puppies should have regular worming medicine under veterinary supervision.

VOMITING is quite a common occurrence in puppies; in fact, they often eat their food very quickly, bring it back up and re-eat it as a natural part of their digestive processes. Eating rough grass often induces vomiting, too, and is generally thought to be beneficial to digestion. A puppy that vomits water as well as food, looks off-colour and cold and also has diarrhoea, is very sick indeed and needs veterinary help without delay.

ZOONOSES are diseases which you and your puppy may catch from one another. Because such diseases do exist you should always wash your hands after handling or playing with your pet. It should have its own bedding and feeding bowls, which must be kept clean and fresh as your own, and you should not allow it to lick your face or hands.

Showing Your Puppy

If you want to show a puppy, it is important to familiarize yourself with all aspects of showing. Visit as many dog shows as you can and keep your eyes and ears open so that you look, listen and learn as much as possible. Join breed clubs and go to their meetings and talks; in this way you will meet breeders and fanciers of the varieties in which you are most interested. Learn all you can about your favourites, and keep a note of the kennels producing consistent winners. Once you know exactly what you want, you are ready to buy your show puppy. You may have to wait for the right puppy, but a reputable kennel with a good winning track record will want you to continue to uphold their reputation and, if you stress that a puppy is for showing, they will only allow you to purchase one of the best. Obviously it is impossible for any kennel to fully guarantee that a small puppy will grow up into a show-stopping champion, but the dedicated breeder will select one with the correct colouring or markings and with typical conformation. Temperament is also very important, for a shy puppy might not show well. Much can happen, too, during the puppy's adolescence, and sometimes a puppy may fail to fulfil its early promise when it gets its second teeth at the age of four to six months and the adult head takes shape.

A show-quality puppy needs basically the same care and feeding as any other puppy. Stick to the breeder's diet sheet and work at building yourself a fit and happy dog. If you have chosen a breed that needs specialized clipping or stripping, make sure that you receive expert tuition and help in carrying this out. Your puppy's breeder is the best person to approach for advice, and may even do the job for you until you have mastered the art yourself.

The show puppy must be accustomed to its grooming routine from a very early age, as the correct presentation can make the difference between winning and losing in the ring. Short-coated dogs are groomed daily and on show days, having been bathed two or three days before, they are polished with a hound glove or silk scarf to bring up the coat's natural sheen. Dogs with heavy coats might need grooming twice a day and probably require a little subtle tidying up of the feathering on the legs and ears. Artificial colouring aids are taboo in the show dog, and it must not be sprayed with any sort of oil or conditioner. Cleaning chalk and dry shampoo powders are allowed, but must be thoroughly removed before the dog enters the ring.

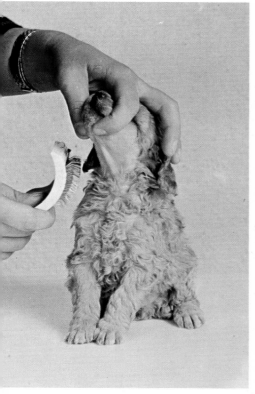

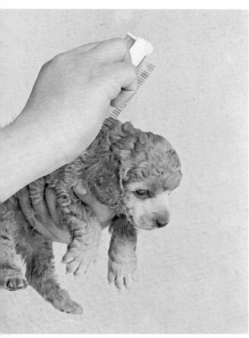

Poodle puppies must be taught to accept regular clipping and grooming routines from a very early age. Left: *Max* clips the face of tiny apricot *Tiopepi Daisy Maid*, destined for a show career. This is followed by a careful grooming. Though she looks a little dejected, she will come to enjoy her beauty sessions and all the extra fuss, attention and praise that goes along with them.

Training is very important and, if possible, you should try to attend some ringcraft classes in your area. Not only will your potential show dog benefit, but you will learn a great deal, too. The classes help to accustom dogs to accept others in quite close proximity and to behave themselves despite the many distractions. You will learn how to present and handle your dog to make the most of its charms. If you are unable to attend such classes, buy instructional books, and watch procedure by attending shows as an observer. Contact the breeder of your puppy for extra help and advice if necessary. Toys and some other small breeds are judged on a table so, if your pet falls into this category, it is essential to get it used to this by placing it on a similar one each day. Stand your puppy on a small table of a convenient height for its daily grooming session and take this opportunity to make it stand up correctly while you examine it in the manner employed by judges. Larger dogs are judged standing on the ground and they must be handled daily, training them to be touched all over their bodies and down their legs without them rolling over in play. It is important that the show dog does not resent any form of handling and will also allow its mouth to be examined by strangers.

Basic training is the same for the show dog as any other puppy but, as lessons progress, specific show training may be introduced. A show dog usually walks on the left side of its handler and you should practise walking together in straight lines and in neat circles. Aim at producing an alert, free-moving walk, with your puppy so eager to please you that it is not easily distracted. Take your puppy with you every time you have to make a short car journey, and make sure that it will allow itself to be benched easily, by tethering it to the leg of the kitchen table for short periods. As training progresses you can tie your puppy's lead to a garden seat or park bench, so that it learns not to resist the tether and that the restriction is only temporary.

If you intend to show your puppy, it is important to choose the best specimen from the litter.

Training should be carried out slowly and methodically. Never tire your puppy out and try to end each training session on a good note, with great praise for a feat well performed. Never try to rush your puppy and always introduce new ideas one at a time. Trying to rush the training might well result in a ring-shy animal, virtually impossible to cure and thus impossible to show.

There are several types of dog shows worldwide, and in Britain there are seven distinct ones. You may well start by entering an Exemption Show of the kind put on for fund-raising by various clubs and charitable organizations. This type of show is exempt from most of the Kennel Club's rules and regulations and, with classes for non-pedigree as well as pedigree dogs, it can be a lot of fun and give you and your novice puppy valuable experience. Primary Shows are confined to breed clubs and have a maximum of eight classes in which first-prize winners are banned from entering. The Match Meeting is exciting, being a sort of knockout competition where dogs meet in couples and are judged against one another until one winner emerges.

Sanction Shows, like the Match Meetings, are confined to club members, and may be for specific breeds or groups of breeds. Limit Shows are also for members only and Challenge Certificate winners are not eligible for competition. Sanction and Limit Shows are the places to gain experience in ringcraft with your puppy. An Open Show is, as its title suggests, open to all and such shows usually have large entries of high quality competitors. The Championship Show may be held specifically for one breed or group of breeds or it may be an all-breed show. Only at this type of show are the coveted Challenge Certificates awarded to the best dog and best bitch of each breed. When a dog or bitch wins three such certificates from three different judges, it is acclaimed as a champion, and may precede its registered name with this title.

There are all manner of classes in which you may be eligible to enter. The PUPPY CLASS is for dogs between the ages of six and twelve calendar months on show day, while the JUNIOR is for dogs between six and eighteen calendar months. The MAIDEN CLASS is for dogs that have not won a Challenge Certificate at any Open or Championship Show except in certain Puppy classes. The NOVICE CLASS is for dogs not having won a Challenge Certificate or three first prizes at Open and Championship Shows, while the UNDERGRADUATE is similarly restricted, but this applies to prizes at Championship shows only. GRADUATE and POST GRADUATE CLASSES gradually allow the dog to elevate its position to entry in the LIMIT CLASSES. The MINOR LIMIT is for dogs with less than two Challenge Certificates and three firsts, the MID LIMIT is for those having won less than three Challenge Certificates and five firsts and the LIMIT is for dogs with less than three Challenge Certificates and seven firsts. In the OPEN CLASS all dogs of the stated breed may enter, while the VETERAN is for older animals, and the BRACE is for two exhibits of the same breed owned by the same person.

In the United States, dog matches differ from dog shows in that points towards Championships and Obedience Degrees are only awarded in the latter. A match provides a wonderful training ground for dogs and their owners; there are Obedience Trials as well as classes judged on conformation, and winners usually receive trophies and ribbons. An American dog show may be a Specialty, which is for dogs of a designated breed, or an All-Breed show, open to all pure-bred registered dogs.

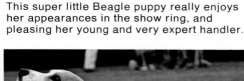

This super little Beagle puppy really enjoys her appearances in the show ring, and pleasing her young and very expert handler.

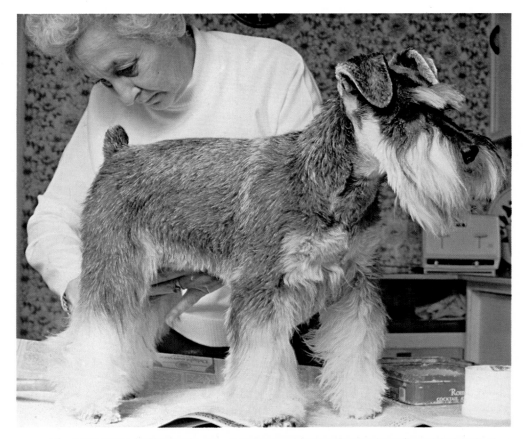

Some breeds need special preparation for the ring. The Miniature Schnauzer is kept well trimmed.

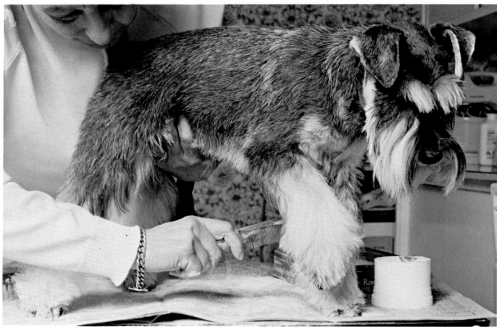

Fine chalk is rubbed into the pale parts of the coat and is then brushed and combed out again.

To win the title of Champion, the American dog must gain 15 points under at least three different judges, and the quantity of points given in each competition is determined by the number of competitors present in the dog's class. Only one male and one female of each breed can win points at any one show, and dogs and bitches never compete against one another.

Dogs competing for Obedience Degrees must score at least 170 points at three different shows and under three different judges, and the rules and regulations for such competitions are complex, testing four distinctly separate levels of training. The lowest level of competence tested in the Obedience Trials is that of Companion Dog and, when this is achieved, owner and dog progress to Companion Dog Excellent. The next test to achieve is that of Utility Dog, and the final difficult and most complicated level of Obedience work is the Utility Dog Tracking.

Field Trials are held for certain breeds and test the abilities of the dog and its owner to work as a co-ordinated team in performing the function for which the specific breed was originally developed. Pointers are required to 'point' effectively, Retrievers are required to recover game and Hounds are required to pursue their quarry, either in packs or in pairs.

You can find out about shows from dog papers and magazines, the breed societies, clubs and your puppy's breeder. Write to the show secretary in good time and enclose a stamped, self-addressed envelope for a show schedule or flyer, which contains all the information you require about rules, entry fees, prizes and lists of classes offered. It also tells you of deadlines for entering and arriving at the show venue and may enclose an entry form which you must complete accurately and return for acceptance prior to show day.

Having entered and been accepted, you must concentrate on building up your dog to show condition with carefully monitored feeding and conditioning, as well as putting the finishing touches to your grooming routine and training programmes. You will also need to decide upon your show equipment and test its suitability for the occasion. You will need an efficient grooming kit and extra cotton wool and tissues to deal with any minor mishaps, containers and bowls for your dog's food and water, and possibly some refreshments for yourself. You need your dog's normal collar and lead for the ring, making sure that it is in very good condition, fits well and has been properly cleaned. On the bench, your dog is tethered by a strong chain conforming to the governing body's rules, and your dog needs a special strong collar to which this may be clipped. The chain is easily adjusted to the correct length, enabling the dog to lie down comfortably, without being able to jump off the bench itself. Toy dogs are provided with enclosed pens on the benching and are not expected to be chained. If you show a breed you may take a flat cushion to give extra comfort to the cage. Larger breeds may have a folded rug or blanket to cushion the hard bench boards.

At smaller shows, dogs do not have to be benched and may stay with their owners throughout the day. It is important, however, to listen out for all announcements concerning classes, as it is possible that times may be changed and you must not miss your own classes.

On show day, leave home in plenty of time so that you do not have to hurry and rush, for this might upset your dog and make it nervous. If your dog should happen to be a little off-colour or there is an outbreak of canine disease in your area or in the vicinity of the show, it is better to forego your outing and keep your pet safely at home.

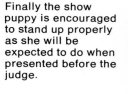
Finally the show puppy is encouraged to stand up properly as she will be expected to do when presented before the judge.

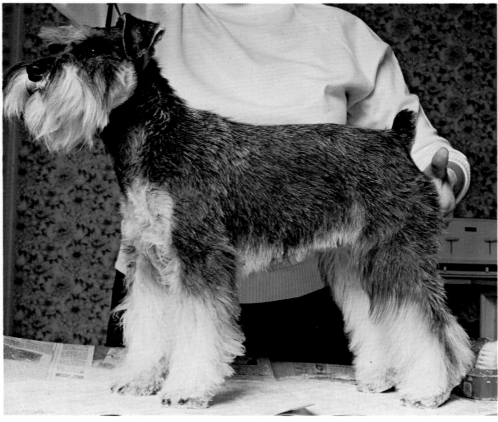

Judges officiate at dog shows and are highly qualified for their job. However, beauty is said to be in the eye of the beholder, and two top judges of a specific breed might not always agree on the finer points and overall presence of a certain exhibit. If you do not do too well in your first show, do not be too despondent. Try again under a different judge – you may have more luck.

The judges are assisted by stewards who call the class number and assemble exhibits in the show ring where they are given identifying numbers. The judge then asks the exhibitors to walk their dogs in a large circle to enable a preliminary assessment of their conformation, manners and movement. After this the exhibitors are asked to line up and the judge then examines each animal separately in turn. The exhibitor must bring his dog forward and pose it in a standing position while the judge passes a critical eye over it, then examines its mouth and general bodily construction. The judge may ask some pertinent questions about the dog which must be answered briefly and politely, but no added information should ever be given.

After the manual examination, the exhibitor is asked to show the dog's action, which is best achieved by walking the animal away from the judge in a perfectly straight line, turning it at the end of the ring and trotting briskly back. This must be done quietly, with discreet commands and the dog's name should not be loudly announced. When each dog has been examined and assessed in this way, the exhibitors line their dogs up, correctly poised once more, while the judge places them in their final winning order.

While it is wonderful to win, and very rewarding to be highly placed, showing must always be considered as fun, and losing not the end of the world. To be successful in the show ring you must also learn to be a good loser, and ready to try again another day. Your dog is not really interested in winning and deserves praise and a rewarding pat for good behaviour, whatever its placing. Be ready to offer sincere congratulations to all the exhibitors whose dogs were placed higher than yours, and equally sincere commiserations to those whose dogs were placed lower.

At the end of the judge's engagement you may approach him to ask about your pet's points. You may find him very tired after his long day of bending, petting and probing, but ready to give you the benefit of his long years of experience with your particular breed. He will point out your dog's good and bad points and may, if you are lucky, give you the one or two little pointers that may turn your good dog into a potential champion.

When the show closes, you should waste no time in packing up and setting off for home, for your dog may be as tired as you are. Give it a good drink on your return, then wipe over its coat and pads with a cloth dipped in a mild disinfectant to destroy any germs possibly picked up at the show. Treat your own shoes in the same way. Give your dog a good feed and allow it to attend to its toilet needs before settling down for a good night's rest, with dreams perhaps of future glories.

Below: It is important for the show dog to remember his manners and to behave well at all times in the ring.

Right: Show dogs must have steady temperaments as shows take place in all manner of venues.

Breeding Puppies

The breeding of dogs should never be undertaken lightly for there are too many unwanted puppies born each year, most of which end up in unsuitable homes, or wait for their inevitable end in the pound. Should you consider dog-breeding as a business, be sure to take expert advice on the relevant licensing laws and be prepared to make a substantial initial capital investment. You will also need expert tuition on the care and maintenance of your breeding stock, whelping and the rearing of puppies, which is probably best learned by a period of work in an established kennel.

As a hobby, dog-breeding can be very interesting if time-consuming. Remember that extra food, stud fees, heating, travelling and veterinary fees are all costly and must be set against any money you might earn on the sales of your litters. If you normally go to work during the day, you will have to take time off from time to time in order to care for your bitch and her litter, and raising puppies can be hard work. If you do decide to breed from your well-bred, happy and healthy bitch, first make sure that you will have homes waiting for all the puppies. Be prepared to provide special facilities for the litter from birth to about ten weeks, where the puppies can be kept warm, quiet and clean. All you have to do then is to find a suitable stud dog and make the necessary arrangements for your bitch to be served when in season.

In the wild, bitches breed once a year, but most domestic dogs have two periods of heat annually and these 'seasons' may be at intervals of six, seven, eight or ten months. A notable exception to this rule is the Basenji which originated in Central Africa and retains the once-yearly breeding cycle of its wild ancestors.

A bitch is not usually bred until her second period of oestrus, or until she is at least eighteen months old. The first signs of heat are seen at the beginning of pro-oestrus when the vulva begins to enlarge and the animal is unusually restless, excited or irritable. A discharge from the vulva may be seen, but is licked away regularly by the bitch who spends extra time in cleaning herself in this region.

The discharge gradually becomes bloodstained and the quantity increases due to the rupturing of tiny blood vessels lining the animal's long vaginal passage, and the vulva itself continues to enlarge and soften. During the nine or ten days of this period, the bitch becomes increasingly attractive to

Below: Draughtproof stables make ideal nurseries for litters of puppies and here the bitch is able to escape from the puppies' attentions when she wishes.

Right: *Oneva Harvest Gold*, a miniature wire-haired dachshund with her fine litter.

male dogs although she is unwilling to mate, and she will start to pass small amounts of urine at frequent intervals as oestrus proper approaches. The bitch is usually mated between the tenth and fifteenth day from the onset of pro-oestrus, or from when the first coloured discharge was seen. You must contact the owner of the stud dog during the pro-oestrus stage and arrange to take your bitch for service on a suitable day during true oestrus. The stud dog's owner will probably want you to assist in the mating by holding your bitch, so you should allow yourself plenty of time. A good stud owner will allow the dogs the opportunity of getting to know one another for a while, and not try to hurry the proceedings. After a successful mating, you will return home with your bitch, and it is important to keep her quiet and indoors away from other dogs until her season is over. You will be expected to pay the stud fee on the day of the mating, and will be given a receipt and a copy of the stud dog's pedigree and registration details.

After mating, the bitch is treated as normal for the first month and will show little or no signs of being pregnant, but during the fifth week her normally slim lines will be seen to thicken and her mammary glands should begin to enlarge. It is possible, too, that she will show signs of nausea in the mornings and her appetite might become rather variable. If it becomes obvious that the bitch has not conceived, then the stud's owner should be contacted, and it is usual for a free return mating to be given at the next season.

A proud West Highland White Terrier bitch with her twins, warm and snug in the stable.

The bitch suckles her puppies and will defend them fiercely if necessary.

During the sixth week, the bitch's diet must be amended to include extra protein and selected vitamins, and this is best done by adding an extra meal instead of increasing the size of her normal meals. Eight weeks after mating the puppies may be seen moving around in the bitch's abdomen while she lies in a relaxed position. She must be kept very fit during her pregnancy and should be given several short, leisurely walks each day. If she becomes constipated, the veterinary surgeon will prescribe a suitable laxative, but in any case it is wise to have him check the bitch over before the puppies are due, and to have him ready to stand by in case of emergency. The gestation period in dogs is nine weeks and the litter size is extremely variable. Small breeds may have two or three puppies while Labradors and Setters often have ten or more youngsters.

Before the puppies are due, prepare a suitable area in which the whelping can take place. It must be warm and quiet, easily cleaned and as dark as possible, but with light available for emergencies. A proper whelping box is ideal, raised from the ground and with a rail inside to prevent the bitch from crushing her puppies as she rolls over. The box should be lined with plenty of clean newspapers and the bitch encouraged to go into the box to rest for a while each day.

Breeding problems do sometimes occur, however, and it may be necessary to call in professional help. Advice should be sought if your bitch goes well over her delivery date but is still obviously pregnant, or if she becomes overly excited and exhibits any strange behaviour patterns. Vigorous straining for two hours without producing a puppy calls for expert attention without further delay. Remember, it is always better to seek advice which later proves unnecessary than to let a potentially dangerous and irrevocable situation develop,

The phenomenon known as a phantom pregnancy sometimes occurs in the bitch. Hormonal changes following a period of heat induce the bitch to act exactly as though she were pregnant. Her abdomen may enlarge, she will produce milk and may fiercely guard some toy or item of clothing, obviously convinced that it is a puppy. This sad state of affairs is best dealt with by giving extra exercise and periods of play, and her bed and surrogate puppies should be removed, but in severe cases it might be necessary to resort to injections of hormones to restore the bitch's normal behaviour.

Puppies soon learn to eat solids and need regular meals of nourishing foods.

In normal pregnancies many bitches have their puppies early, so watch your pet carefully towards the end of her pregnancy. The first signs of labour are marked restlessness and a refusal to eat, followed by very deep and nervous panting. During this initial stage, which can last for up to twelve hours and may be exhausting for you as well as your bitch, the mammary glands become active, the pelvic ligaments soften and the vulva enlarges. The bitch may feel quite cold as her body temperature drops, and her uterus will start its first mild contractions.

Eventually the bitch enters the preparation stage of labour and the contractions of the uterus can be felt by resting your hand on her abdomen. During this stage the position of the first puppy that will be born is changed: it rotates, safely enclosed within its amniotic sac, and begins its journey through the cervix and vagina towards the outside world. This stage usually lasts from three to six hours, although it is not uncommon for it to be extended to twenty-four hours, and during it the contractions are quite irregular.

Finally, very regular contractions start and the bitch holds her breath at the end of each one, using the muscles of her diaphragm and abdomen until a sac of dark fluid is expelled. This is quickly followed by the first puppy, still enclosed within its own sac. The bitch will lick the membranes from her baby's face, stimulating it to take its first breath of air, then lick away the rest of the sac. The afterbirth is generally expelled with the puppy or after another contraction, and is eaten by the bitch, along with the umbilical cord up to a point about an inch or two from the puppy's navel. While she cleans and tends her puppy, further contractions produce the next youngster, which is dealt with in a similar fashion.

The puppies should be delivered in a warm, draught-free environment and, if the bitch cannot cope with the cleaning and drying, then you must be prepared to take over, for more puppies die of neonatal-cold injury – that is, chilling immediately after birth – than of any other single cause. You may provide an infra-red lamp hung over the whelping box to provide extra heat at this critical time, or you may prefer to have ready a warm pad of special polyester fur fabric into which you can tuck each puppy as you dry if off after birth. You may have to leave the firstborn with the bitch in order to keep her settled in the whelping box, and its suckling should help hormone changes to occur in the bitch's body, speeding up the delivery of subsequent puppies. In any event do not remove the pups any distance from the whelping box, and sit near to the bitch, helping when necessary and keeping as quiet and calm as possible.

In a normal birth, puppies are born at forty-minute intervals, and when the last one has arrived the bitch is seen to relax and settle down with her new family. Once you have assured yourself that there are no more youngsters to come, and that all the afterbirths have been safely delivered, you may clean the bitch up by wiping her hindquarters with a soft cloth wrung out in hand-hot water. Dry her carefully, and pull out all the wettest and most heavily soiled paper from the nextbox. Tuck handfuls of soft paper towelling under her if she is reluctant to leave the bed, otherwise you can put a clean pad of polyester fur or folded flannelette sheeting in her bed.

Most bitches really appreciate a warm nourishing drink at this stage and you may find that she will take eggs beaten into warm milk with added glucose. Encourage her to drink, check that all is well, then leave the little family to rest in peace and quiet.

The puppies are born with eyes tight shut and are unable to hear. They scrabble on weak legs towards the warmth of their mother's body and

Tiopepi Golden Daisy, an apricot miniature Poodle bitch, proudly displays her lovely, even litter.

attach themselves to her full teats where they receive the important substance called colostrum. This contains antibodies against all the diseases that the bitch has encountered during her life, plus antibodies produced by the vaccines with which she has been inoculated. The bitch makes a considerable quantity of rich milk which is secreted by the mammary glands after the colostrum has been drawn off by the puppies, and they will feed from her for about six weeks, although they are able to supplement her milk with solid foods between the third to fourth week of their lives.

One critical period in the young puppies' lives is the first five days, during which their bodies are learning to adapt from the warmth and comfort of life inside the womb. The outside world has less constant conditions, and the little creatures have to undergo considerable functional changes in their circulatory and respiratory systems. Their excretions are stimulated by the licking of their dam's tongue. The bitch requires double her normal food intake during lactation, and even with unlimited quantities of food she may look very thin by the time her litter reaches three weeks of age. Around this time she will quite possibly regurgitate some partially digested food to encourage her puppies to eat. This is quite normal, and copies behaviour patterns observed in wild-dog packs.

For some weeks after whelping the bitch may have a discharge from her vulva which starts as a thick dark emission, then gradually turns to a clear red. The larger the litter, the more discharge may be expected as it is comes from the areas where the placentas were attached inside the uterus. If the discharge looks or smells unpleasant at any time, you should seek veterinary help, as this could indicate a retained placenta, or even a dead puppy.

Although puppies are able to lap liquids at three weeks and eat their first solid foods by the age of four weeks, the bitch will continue to feed them until they are six or seven weeks old. She should never be shut in with the

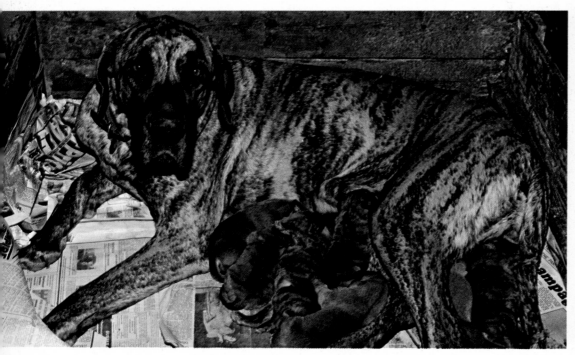

puppies, however, as they will not leave her alone and will worry her with their sharp little teeth at a time when she is beginning to feel rather run down. Puppies are quite easy to wean and must be given easily digested food in very small quantities at frequent intervals.

Sometimes puppies have to be delivered surgically through the abdominal wall. This operation is known as a Caesarean section and is performed whenever a bitch is unable to produce her young in the normal way. The cause may be the presence of a mummified foetus or two or a dead puppy blocking the birth canal, or her pelvic passages may be too small to allow the passage of the live puppies. If such an operation is called for, it is performed in the veterinary surgery under a general anaesthetic, and you will be contacted and allowed to collect your bitch and her babies, once she has regained full consciousness. The bitch may take a little longer to

Above left: Newborn Dane puppies of the Nollybob strain in their wooden whelping box under an infra-red heating lamp.

accept and feed her puppies if they are delivered in this way, and she should be kept as quiet and warm as possible until she settles down with them. If her milk does not come in quickly, you may need to hand-feed the puppies from a bottle fitted with a teat of suitable size.

If you do have to hand-rear a litter of puppies because a bitch's milk supply fails or is inadequate, or if she tragically dies giving birth, the puppies' first feed should be of a glucose solution. This is made by dissolving 1 oz (25 g) of glucose in 1 pt (600 ml; U.S. 2½ cups) of boiled water. Healthy puppies soon perk up when fed this every hour or two, and may then progress to regular four-hourly milk feeds. Depending on the size and breed of the puppies, you can feed them with an eyedropper, a plastic syringe, a human baby's bottle or a calf-feeding bottle. Special milk powder should be bought for feeding puppies, but in an emergency cows' milk can be used and

Above: Until they are house trained, puppies are best kept on an absorbent floor of newspapers or straw, so that they stay clean and fresh.

evaporated cows' milk diluted with an equal quantity of boiled water is even better. Remember that cows' milk is not as rich as bitch's milk, so never dilute it, but rather enrich it by adding a beaten raw egg or some full cream milk powder.

Orphan puppies must be kept in a room temperature of around 100°F (38°C) just after birth, but after five days this may be reduced to 75°F (24°C) if they are progressing well. They must be kept clean and stimulated to pass urine and faeces after every meal. This is done by gently wiping the genital areas with a stroking motion, using a warm, damp piece of cotton wool, copying the natural cleaning motions of the bitch. Weigh the puppies every day and make sure that their progress follows the normal weight curve for their breed. Such puppies will probably have missed the benefit of the antibodies provided in their mother's first milk, the colostrum, and therefore your veterinary surgeon might consider it advantageous to vaccinate them at an earlier age than usual. Be guided in this by his past experience and take his advice.

In naturally reared and hand-reared litters, weaning is usually begun when the litter is about three weeks old by offering the puppies a meal of milk made up to a creamy consistency by the addition of some sort of baby cereal. Warm food is more acceptable than cold food at this stage, and the puppies are introduced to the new taste by licking your fingers that have been dipped into the paste. The procedure is repeated regularly every four hours until the puppies learn to lap, then, in their fourth week, two of the milky feeds are replaced with two of finely minced and scraped meat, or a proprietary brand of puppy food. The bitch should be separated from the puppies at least an hour before they are fed, and only allowed back in their pen after they have eaten their fill. In this way they will learn to eat more and more food from their bowls and take less from their dam, so that her milk supply gradually diminishes quite naturally.

Every breeder has his or her pet theory about weaning, but it is really a matter of common sense during a time when you are eager to do your best for both bitch and puppies. The most important thing is to make sure that all your little dogs are receiving an adequately balanced diet with no deficiencies which might give rise to later health problems.

A litter of Cocker Spaniel puppies from the Bidston kennels; three dainty, winsome bitches and a larger sturdy little dog.